AN ORDINARY SAINT

AN ORDINARY SAINT

SAINT

The Life of
John Neumann

By JANE F. HINDMAN

An Associates for Hope Publication
Society of the Divine Savior
Salvatorian Center, WI 53062

ARENA LETTRES • NEW YORK

Nihil Obstat: James McGrath
                  Censor Librorum

Imprimatur: ✠ John Cardinal Krol
                  Archbishop of Philadelphia

Philadelphia, Pennsylvania, 21 March, 1977

AN ORDINARY SAINT

Printed in the United States of America

Library of Congress Catalog Card No. 77-075429

ISBN: 0-88479-004-5

For my nephews,
George and Owen,
Michael, Stephen,
Joseph, Christopher,
and their sisters
with my love.

FOREWORD

A saint is a person to whom God has given the strength to take the commandment of love of God and of man with utter seriousness, to understand it profoundly and to use every effort to carry it out. As simple as this may sound, it nonetheless demands a reorientation of life, or purpose, of energy and ambition in the person who accepts seriously the divine command. A saint is one who goes forward to meet God's command resolutely and completely, without reservation.

The manner in which love unfolds distinguishes one saint from another. The lives of the saints continue to have a mysterious attraction upon us for each of them clearly demonstrated that sanctity is sublime indeed and worth the trouble anytime. The saints, as human as we are, and subject to human limitations, have proved beyond doubt that the rung of a ladder was never meant to rest upon, but only to hold a man's foot long enough to enable him to put the other higher.

How abundantly fulfilled was the divine command in the life of Saint John Neumann is very simply, yet beautifully, described in this work by Jane Hindman. This volume with its lucid and interesting style and its wise selection of interesting events will surely broaden the spectrum of sanctity.

JOHN CARDINAL KROL

CONTENTS

CHAPTER ONE

LIFE IN A WALLED TOWN

OVER THE GATE of the ancient town of Prachatitz hung the portrait of an eleventh-century lord. To four-year-old John Neumann standing in the square and looking up at the fierce warrior astride a white horse, it was the most exciting picture in the world.

"Tell me again, Mother. What do the words under it say?"

"We praise old times, but we live in the present," his mother read for him.

"When will I be able to read those words for myself?"

"When you are seven you will go to school and learn to read."

"That is a long time to wait." He tried to spell out some of the letters.

"It will come soon enough." His mother smiled at the earnest little boy. "Come along now, we do not want to be late for church."

John thought Prachatitz a most wonderful town. It was very old. At one time, possibly in the eleventh century, it had been the center of trade between Bohemia and Bavaria. The streets had

been built narrow and crooked to keep large
armies from marching through. Unfortunately,
they had not deterred hordes of warriors who
descended on the town. The walls of the city
showed signs of battle, as did the church of Saint
James.

To remind the townsfolk of their history, fres-
coes had been painted on the walls of the large
buildings surrounding the square. The meaning
of the pictures had been explained to John so
often that he knew them by heart. The town
had been the scene of bloody battles during the
religious wars.

Gradually, Prachatitz lost its importance and
became a peaceful, small, walled town with its
share of joy and sadness. But wars still raged in
other parts of Europe. To escape them, Philip
Neumann had come from Germany in 1802 and
in a two-story brick house on one of the narrow
streets had set up his looms for knitting stockings.
He was a friendly man. Neighbors passing by
would often stick their heads in the window to
greet him or to watch the deft fingers of the
knitters as they worked at their looms.

In the town, Philip met a Czech girl. They
married and set up family life. Before long they
had two daughters, Catherine and Veronica. Both
parents were religious and loving and they trained
their children well. John, the third child, was born
on March 28, 1811. That same day, his god-
parents took him down the street to the church
of Saint James and, with his sisters Catherine and
Veronica looking on, he was baptized and given

the name of the patron saint of Bohemia, John Nepomucene.

The two little girls loved to play with their baby brother even though he was not the baby of the family for long. He had been replaced by Joan, then Louise, and last of all by their brother Wenceslaus, whom they always called Wenzel.

John soon found that there were many things for a little boy to discover. Before long, he learned that beyond the city walls there were the fields of the family farm in which he could run and play to his heart's content. Then, as he grew, his father took him on walks up the surrounding mountains. From on high they could look down on the walled city. John thought how well protected and secure it looked, as though those who lived there were surrounded by the arms of God.

To his father's great pleasure, John, while still a toddler, would stand for a long time beside the looms listening to their whir and watching the stockings grow under the fingers of the workmen.

"He will follow in my footsteps," thought Philip, "and will make a name for himself in Prachatitz."

It was, however, only the motion of the looms that fascinated the child; he knew he did not want to sit in front of them himself.

"Please take me to the town square," he would beg his sisters when he was too young to be allowed to go by himself. There he would stand looking at the pictures of men and horses on the walls of the city buildings.

At last he was allowed to go alone to the square.

While he looked at the paintings, he longed to be
able to read about the scenes they depicted. Often
he would slip into Saint James Church to ask the
Dear Lord to help him to grow up fast so he could
go to school to learn as much as he could. There
were so many things that he needed to know.

The church was the hub of the town of Prachatitz. The citizens often dropped in to say a prayer,
and many of them attended Mass each morning.
Mrs. Neumann was often among them, frequently
accompanied by one or two of her children.

One Friday, in the autumn of 1816, the sun
was rising behind the church when she and two
of her children walked down its steps.

"Hurry, children," she said, "Mass was a bit
late this morning and our friends will be waiting
for us."

Five-year-old John skipped beside his mother,
grasping her full skirt. "The bread smelled good
when we left home," he said.

"Maria was about ready to take it from the
oven. It should be cool enough to handle by now,"
replied his mother as they hurried down the
street and turned in at their door. Already there
was a line of about twenty people waiting at
their window.

The poor in the city of Prachatitz had learned
that it was Frau Neumann's custom to give bread
on Friday, her baking day, to all who were in
need.

"John, you and Veronica may help me today,"
said his mother as she took off her shawl.

Both children ran to get the baskets of bread

the maid had filled, and between them carried them to their mother who was talking to the first people in line.

Turning to the little boy, she said, "Mrs. Schmidt's father is sick again, please give her two loaves."

With a shy smile, the little boy handed the crusty brown loaves to the woman, who was profuse in her thanks.

After she had given to all who applied, Mrs. Neumann closed the window and turned to the two children. "When we see all those poor sick people, we should thank God for all our blessings."

"Yes, mother," both agreed soberly. They thought there was much suffering in their town.

One Friday evening as John and his sisters sat around the dinner table with their parents, his father said:

"Frau Neumann, I hope we have seen the last of your bread line."

The whole family looked in astonishment at their father seated so comfortably at the head of the table. What did he mean? Always so generous, had he suddenly decided that he no longer wanted to share a crust of bread?

As Mr. Neumann saw how worried the family looked, he smiled at them. "Come, now, you don't think I've changed that much?"

"No, sir," piped John. "But, but, Papa, what will the poor people do?"

"That is what I am trying to tell you," said his father, ruffling the little boy's hair. "Today, at the Town Council, I was appointed Prefect of the Poor, and I plan to see that no one is in need of bread."

A sigh of relief was heard all around the table, and all sorts of questions were put to Mr. Neumann until he covered his ears and begged for mercy.

True to his word, Philip Neumann took such good care of the poor that there were no beggars left in the town. For many years, he performed his work so well that the town kept re-appointing him to office, and his family was proud of his kindness and love of the poor.

Living in such a household, it was no wonder that John grew in thoughtfulness for others.

At long last the day for which he had been hoping for so long arrived. John was to begin school and to learn to read.

Most of the seven-year-olds in his class were bigger than he. They were boisterous in their play and some tried to bully the little boy who was shy and did not often enter into their games. But when they saw how quickly he learned and how ready he was to help them, they let him alone.

When he had learned to read, John's father gave him a bookcase of his own. Few children in the 1800s could boast of owning a bookcase. To fill it, he gathered all the books in the house, and then set out to read them. Some of them were very difficult, as his father was a great reader on many subjects. Undaunted, he struggled to spell out the big words, and to understand what they meant. He formed the habit of getting up at five each morning, summer or winter, hot or cold, so he could have extra time to read.

One day his mother asked, "John, why do you get up so early each day?"

"Because I have so much reading to do. I can't find enough time to do it."

"But son," she replied, "you don't have to learn everything at once. You have years before you."

In his serious way he answered, "But, I do not know when I'll die, and I may not have finished reading my books."

His mother laughed, but shook her head in wonder at their brown-eyed son.

In those days, boys who were going into business attended school for only six years, and were then apprenticed to learn a trade. John desperately wanted to continue his studies, but knew the decision was to be made by his parents. At last the time had come when the boy's future must be decided; if he were to consider a trade, his father would have to look for someone who would be willing to take him in his workshop.

One evening, Frau Neumann invited the pastor and the schoolmaster to dinner. John knew this was no ordinary invitation. His mother and father wanted advice from these good men about the future education of their son.

After a hearty meal, all the children except John were excused and sent to play. His father began to speak.

"It seems to me, sirs, that my son has no interest in my business, but would profit by more education."

John sat quietly looking from one to another as they spoke.

"He has a fine mind, sir," said the schoolmaster, "and is serious in his studies."

"What would you like to be, John?" asked the pastor, turning to the young boy.

"Sir," answered John, "I am not sure, but I do not want to be a knitter." Seeing the disappointment on his father's face, he added quickly, "Papa, not that I wouldn't like to be good and kind like you, but I want to do something that I can study and think about."

At that time there were few professions open. He could be a lawyer, doctor, teacher, or priest, but the child did not yet know which of these he would like to be. Maybe he could be a teacher. He gave only passing thought to the other professions, as they would cost his father too much money.

After a few minutes of discussion, his father said: "It looks as though the votes for the school at Budweis are all in, and to tell the truth, I will be proud of my son when he becomes a professor."

"But sir," John stood up and faced his teacher. "Do you think I can pass the entrance examination?"

"I am starting a night class in Latin. You should join."

"We will talk of that later," said his father. "For the present, John, I think you should go to your lessons."

John bowed to each of the guests and to his

father, hugged his mother and ran from the room.

For two years, John studied Latin and did well in his classes. In the meantime he was reading as much as he could. When the time came for the examinations, he had no trouble in passing them. Although he knew he would miss his family very much, he was delighted to know that in the fall he would be in Budweis.

CHAPTER TWO

STUDENT DAYS

THAT SUMMER in the Neumann household
there was a mingling of pride at John's success
and sadness that he would be going from home.
Budweis was only fifteen miles away, but at that
time the best way to get there was to walk.
Fifteen miles each way was too far for a twelve-
year-old boy to travel each day, even though he
was accustomed to long hikes in the mountains.

At last the day came when his mother said,
"John, it is now time to gather your clothes
together. Your father has made arrangements for
you to stay with Mr. Eberle. You will not be
lonely as several other boys are boarding with
him."

John wondered briefly about this arrangement,
as he would need a quiet place to study. Would
the others want to study when he did? He put
the thought aside as his mother and the maid
started to pack the big yellow trunk that the workmen had brought down from the attic. Into it
went his books, his microscope, and a good
supply of clothing. The top layer was then filled

with bread, cheese, cookies and a bag of apples and nuts. At last all was ready, and the day of departure arrived. His mother and sisters cried as they kissed him good-bye and the workmen hoisted the now heavy trunk onto the wagon that his father had hired to take him and several other boys to Budweis.

What wonders they were to see in the city of Budweis. It was the capital of the province, and the center of commerce for southern Bohemia. Ships traveled on both the Malse and Vlatva Rivers. And, although the boys could scarcely believe it, there was a railway that connected the cities of Budweis and Linz. Before he took them to their boarding house, Mr. Neumann drove the boys around the big square and took them to see the wooden rails that seemed to run on forever. They would have to wait for another day to see the horse-drawn train. When they reached Mr. Eberle's house they all tumbled out and thanked Mr. Neumann. Future trips would have to be made on foot.

The boys shouted and shoved each other as they ran up the stairs to see their room, John turned to his father to thank him and kiss him good-bye.

"We expect great things of you, my son," said his father, with a catch in his voice.

"I will try, Papa, I will try," he replied, making an effort to smile, but as the boys' voices came down to him, he could not help but wonder how he would fare.

John was so well prepared that he could have gone directly into the third year of his high school course, but that was not allowed.

Their teacher was so lazy that no one studied. Most of the boys spent their time getting into mischief in the town.

"Come along, John," they would say, but John knew that they did not mean it. He would not share in their fun.

One day when his sister Catherine came for a visit, he complained, "I am not learning a thing. This teacher is kind enough, but he is a poor teacher. I spend my days in reading."

It took the authorities eighteen months to find out what John could have told them in three days. The teacher was dismissed. His successor tried to make up for lost time and worked the class very hard. In spite of these problems, John passed his examination.

For three years he did very well. Then came his fourth and final year before going to college. This year was a great trial to him. He had changed his boarding house, but not for the better. The son of his landlady took such delight in teasing and disturbing John that he could not study, and his marks fell. Discouraged, he returned home, feeling that he may have been meant to be a stocking knitter after all, and that he had wasted enough time.

When he showed his report to his father, his parent was of the same opinion. Frowning over the report, he said, "John, you seem no longer interested in your studies. You may stay home and choose a trade!"

With tears in her eyes, his mother watched both her husband and son. Later she talked to her daughter Veronica.

"Do you think it right for John to give up his studies?" she asked.

"Oh no, Mamma. This is John's whole life. He'll never be happy with a trade. Can't you get Papa to change his mind?"

"If I do, will John agree to return to Budweis?" wondered Mrs. Neumann.

"Yes, Mamma, yes, John can be persuaded easily. He is feeling so badly now because of his poor marks, and I do not think they are his fault. For some reason, the professor did not like him."

A few evenings later, as Mr. Neumann was reading and Mrs. Neumann was working on some fine embroidery, she looked up, and seeing her husband staring into space, asked, "Is something troubling you, Philip?"

"It is John. He seems so worried and unhappy."

"I know," sighed his mother. "It is that wretched report. We are making a great mistake in allowing our son to give in to his discouragement."

"But you saw the report. He did not do well this year."

"Have you asked him for any explanation? Somehow I do not feel that those marks give a clear picture of what he has learned."

"What else can I go on?" asked his father.

"Today I heard that a professor from the college is visiting our pastor. Why not speak to him?"

"I will do that," said Philip, picking up his book with the air of having solved a great problem.

Mr. Neumann did speak to the professor, who sent for John and questioned him at great length. Then he called on John's father. "Your son has a fine mind. He has a good grasp of the subjects he has studied, and a wide knowledge beside. Should you not send him to college, in my opinion, you would be making a great mistake."

Mr. Neumann, thus encouraged, agreed to send John back to his studies. It remained only for John's mother and Veronica to persuade him to return. This year he had a room of his own in a quiet house without distractions and his marks immediately improved.

During his two years of college, John was interested in many subjects and seemed readily to find experts who would instruct him. He made friends with Joseph Juttner, an artillery commander who explained higher mathematics in such a way that his marks soared.

Anton Laad had been a friend since his early school days, but now he added to his intimate circle Adalbert Schmidt and Karl Krbecek. While all were interested in science, each had a special field. John from early childhood had been fascinated by the stars. He now added an interest in botany. It was the habit of one or two of the boys to tramp the countryside in all kinds of weather to search for specimens of plants. When they returned, they always found the others waiting in John's room to look at their finds and to discuss the experiments the others had been conducting. In this way, each broadened his knowledge.

Not all their time was spent in study, however. Always hungry, Anton or one of the others would look longingly at the big yellow trunk. From past experience they knew what it held.

"Has Veronica been here lately?" asked Anton one day as they sat around talking.

"Now let me see if I can remember," John replied.

Adalbert interrupted, "Come, John, none of your teasing. I saw her here yesterday. Did she leave anything?"

Eager hands lifted the lid.

"Adalbert, do have a piece of the sausage," said John laughing, for Adalbert already had it in his hand, his knife ready to cut a slice.

"Here is a piece of cheese to make it taste better," said Anton.

"What would you do with all this food if we were not here to help you?" asked Karl between bites of a russet apple.

"I don't know. Mother insists I eat my dinner out, and all I need for breakfast and supper is a slice of mother's good brown bread."

When all were satisfied, John pulled his guitar out from under the bed and the boys sat around singing. After they had sung many of the familiar songs, Karl said, "Let's sing one in Italian."

"Who knows Italian around here?" asked Anton.

Karl said, "What, you've missed something? John has been teaching me Italian and I've been teaching him Czech."

"All right," grumbled Adalbert, "Anton and I will listen to you two while you sing your songs, then I have studying to do. I must be off."

The two years of philosophy passed quickly. The friends who towered over John found him the center of their group. They all decided that it was important to continue their studies. Doctor, lawyer, teacher, priest? Which of these professions should they choose? Unlike many boys away from home, John had continued attending Mass daily, said his prayers faithfully, and visited the Blessed Sacrament in the church in the evening. Otherwise he showed no signs of piety.

Since he had amassed a great knowledge of flowers and ferns in his rambles, he thought maybe he would be a botany professor. His father thought that he might be a doctor and was willing to send him to Prague to study. But somehow John could not settle in his decision for his future. His return from college in 1831 was quite different from that two years earlier. He had graduated with distinction. This time there was no question of his completing his studies. His father would make further sacrifices to educate his son.

John, a small but sturdy young man, spent many hours worrying about what God wanted him to do.

One day, he sat watching his mother so placidly knitting.

"Mother," he said.

"Yes, son?" Mrs. Neumann put her work in her lap to give her son her full attention.

"Mother," he began again, "I do appreciate all that you and father have sacrificed for me, but here I am twenty and know no more what I want to do than at the age of ten."

His mother looked at him thoughtfully. "I can't quite believe that, John. Even though you think it impossible, you show every sign of wanting to be a priest."

John looked at his mother in amazement. "How could you know that? I haven't even dared to say it to myself."

"Mothers know more than they are given credit for," she remarked, smiling gently.

Talking half to himself, John continued, "How could I have been so blind? All along I seem to have leaned that way, but what a great deal of time I have wasted on other interests. Now, I know and it is too late."

"Don't say that, son." Stuffing her knitting into her bag, she rose and said, "We will go tell your father your decision."

John put a restraining hand on her arm.

"Not so fast, Mother. You know that the seminary is overcrowded and that the authorities are very strict. Only those who have the best recommendations from well-known men even have a chance. I know no one to speak for me. Already eighty have applied, but only twenty will be accepted."

"No one to speak for you?" For once his mother sounded stern. "The Good Lord will speak for you if He wants you to be His priest. Your part is to take the examination and to pass. Then it will be out of your hands. You will take the examination, John, won't you?"

Smiling at her faith and vehemence, John took his hand from her arm and followed her in search of his father.

Mr. Neumann, somewhat bewildered at the turn of events, readily agreed to financing John's further studies. So John took the examination and although there were four applicants for every opening in the seminary, John Neumann's marks were so outstanding that he was accepted without question. Although he was astounded, his mother was not surprised.

CHAPTER THREE

DECISION

ACCEPTED in the seminary with John were his childhood friend Anton Laad and Adalbert Schmidt, who was to become his confidant. Since there was no room at the seminary for new students, John roomed across the street.

"Did you bring your yellow trunk?" asked Anton.

"Yes, but I finally persuaded my mother that we are no longer growing boys and do not need so much food. A little fasting will do you good."

Anton groaned, "Oh, well, we'll come and study with you, anyway."

Many evenings the young men gathered to study Italian and French and to improve their knowledge of Scripture by firing questions at one another. By the end of the first year, John had made extensive notes on the Bible. He also learned Hebrew so that he could read Scripture in that language.

Days passed quickly at the seminary. At the close of the year, the president called John into his office and said, "You know that at the end of the first year of seminary study, we only allow one or two to take minor orders, the first step to priesthood."

"Yes, sir," said John. This was not news. He wondered who was to be so honored.

Since it never occurred to him that he would be selected, he was astounded when the president continued: "You have been one of those chosen to receive these orders."

John could scarcely express his thanks. He was delighted, not because he thought he deserved the honor, but because he thought it would hasten the day he would become a priest. He was still the little boy who was always pushing ahead to the next goal.

During the period that John Neumann was so concerned with his books, great things were happening in that vast land across the ocean called America. The progress made in those lands was scarcely noted by the people in Bohemia. To them, this was a country of war whoops and Indian scalpings — a vast untamed wilderness. They did not realize that thousands of immigrants were encouraged to go to America to till the land and to work on the canals and railroads that were being built in the 1820s. Cheap labor was needed and these poor people were being exploited. Many of them were German-speaking Catholics who were going to a land alien in both language and religion. They must be helped. A missionary, Father Résé, came to Austria to beg for funds and persuaded the emperor to establish the Leopoldine Missionary Society for the aid of the

German-speaking people in America. The faithful were encouraged to contribute money to the missions. It did not occur to them to send priests.

John read the quarterly reports of the Leopoldine Missionary Society. They often included letters from Father Baraga, called the "Apostle of the Chippewas." The young man's heart was touched by the needs of the immigrants.

To cap his interest, he was profoundly moved by a lecture delivered by Professor Koerner on Saint Paul and his missionary activities. "If Saint Paul, a little man like me, but not as strong as I am, could do so much, why can't I become a missionary in America?" he asked himself.

Of course he could, and to prepare for such an arduous life, John began immediately to eat as little as possible and to harden his body by exposing it to every kind of weather.

A mountain boy, John was used to walking long distances. He increased the length of his walks, and shortened his hours of sleep. When his friends asked for the reason for the change in his habits, he merely shrugged them off.

One day, as John and Adalbert were on a long hike, they sat to eat their lunch of bread and cheese. Adalbert broke the silence by blurting out, "John, I have something to tell you. I've decided that after ordination, I will become a missionary to America."

To Adalbert's surprise, John took the news calmly, and questioned him on what he planned to do.

"So you want to be a pioneer? Do you know how to get on a horse, much less ride one? How will you talk to the Indians?"

For a short time, he teased Adalbert, then one day he said, "Your idea did not surprise me, as for some time I have been planning the same thing. Possibly we can go together."

Both young men felt more courage to go to the wilds of America if they had a friend at hand. They also knew that in preparation for their mission they would have to know more languages than their German and Czech. After all, in the cities of America, English was spoken. It was only where groups of Germans had gathered that they would hear their own language. So they set themselves to learning English and making themselves more proficient in French. Anton Laad, who was interested, but would not commit himself, suggested to John, "If only we could go to the seminary at Prague, we would be able to attend classes in English and French."

Always careful not to ask for special privileges, John hesitated: "Would the rector permit us to go?"

"The seminary always sends two or three students up to the city for their third and fourth years of study. Why not us?" asked Anton.

"But I'm sure there are others who should go before us."

"Bosh, John. Why not us? We are as good in our studies as the others. Come, we'll go ask right now."

To John's surprise, the rector agreed. The

Neumann family were excited when they heard
the news. Prague was a large city and John would
have many adventures there, they were sure. With
their parents' blessings and admonitions ringing
in their ears, John and Anton took the coach to
Prague.

The great city was quite bewildering to the
two young men from the mountains. Streets in
the older part of town were crooked and narrow,
as they were at home, but many more people
were packed into them. The new section of the
city had wide tree-lined avenues, many parks,
larger buildings than John had ever seen, and
perched on the hills surrounding the city were
too many castles to count.

The university stretched on the right bank of
the river in the old section of town. It accom-
modated thousands of students. The seminary,
one small portion of the university, was housed in
the second largest building in town — second
only to the Imperial Palace. In it were classrooms
and living quarters for the 150 theological students. For the first time in his life, John was to
live with his fellow students under discipline. The
rules for the seminary students were rigid. John
and Anton were not allowed to attend classes
in French. There were no classes in English.
Added to that, they found some of the professors
were not as learned, nor as good teachers as those
in Budweis. They were discouraged and dis-
appointed. They would have to continue their
studies on their own.

One free afternoon, John went for a walk. He

was thinking about his problems, when he heard some voices coming from the open door of a factory. He poked his head in the door and found there were several men talking to one another in English. They turned to look at the serious young man in cassock and round hat standing in the doorway.

"Can I help you sir?" asked the foreman respectfully.

"I thought I heard you speaking English."

"That is right, we are from England, and we hear our own language only in this workroom."

"I wanted to speak to you about that," said John eagerly. "I need to know English, and I cannot find anyone to help me. May I come and talk to you men?"

They glanced at one another. They knew no Catholic priest in their own country. What would he want with the likes of them? Was he making fun of them?

John, seeing them hesitate, said, "You see, I plan to go to America as a missionary, and I must know English."

"Don't you know, little man, those Indians could shoot an arrow straight through you?" The foreman looked hard at John, then laughed. "I'll tell you what you do. Just stand sidewise and there will be nothing to hit."

Seeing that John took their teasing in good part, one man said, "Oh, let him come. This work is dull enough. We can use some laughs. Come when you can."

"I will be able to come see you only on Tues-

d.y and Thursday afternoons. They are my only
free hours," he said.

"They do keep you busy. We will look for
you then."

It was fortunate that the president of the
seminary never came to that part of town, or he
would have been shocked to see John, his sleeves
rolled back, working with the men as they talked.

While the regulations forbade John to attend
French classes, he studied on his own and asked
to take the examination at the end of the term.
He passed with distinction.

But at the seminary, he was having a difficult
time. Some of the subjects were not taught as they
should have been, causing John to do much re-
search and to dispute some of the teaching of his
professors. He could not feel close to the president
of the seminary, who should have been his spiritual advisor. He began to write a spiritual journal
which he continued from time to time until he
became a Redemptorist priest. In this he recorded
his feelings of loneliness, abandonment, and un-
worthiness to be a priest. Many nights he did not
sleep because of his worries. Daily he grew in
humility.

The liberal students at the seminary looked
on John with contempt. One evening in study
hall one of these students read a paper about
"our altar boy who has such ridiculously rigid
opinions."

Anton was indignant. "What are you going to
do, John? Whatever you decide to do, I'll help
you. We must stop this."

"No," said John. "I'll just be as kind to them as I know how. The only damage done is to my pride. They really have done me a favor."

Nevertheless, he was happy when vacation time rolled around and he was able to go home. While he did not mention either America or his difficulties at Prague, his mother knew he had much on his mind.

Before he had to return to the seminary, he met Adalbert Schmidt.

"Father Hermann Dichtl," said Adalbert, "is my confessor. He knows all about our plans for America."

"What does he think?" asked John. "I have not told the president of my seminary yet."

"Father Dichtl will help us all he can. He is trying to encourage the Leopoldine Foundation to begin a seminary for missionaries. If they do not do that, he hopes they will send priests to America."

"Meaning us?"

"Yes. I will let you know how things turn out." With their hopes high, the friends parted for their last year of study before ordination.

On their return journey to Prague, Anton Laad insisted that they had an obligation to tell the president of their desire for missionary work.

"I can't understand you, John. You always do the right thing. I am still considering going, but you are really determined to go. He should be told."

"Then you tell him, Anton. He is always busy when I ask to see him."

Shortly after they were settled, Anton poked his head in John's room. "I told the president about us and he said nothing. So I guess he does not object."

A few days later, John was sitting in the museum reading, when the president approached him. Abruptly he said, "Are you serious in your intention to be a missionary?"

"Yes, sir, but I do not wish it to be generally known," answered John, rising to speak to his superior.

The priest turned and left without another word. Bewildered, John sat down, wondering what he had done to make the president wish to avoid him. "He seems to despise me," thought John, and decided it would not be right to consult another, so he would have to keep silent about his intention.

A few days later the president met him in the hall, and suggested that he join the Jesuits. John was not inclined to accept this suggestion. He thought if he, a secular priest, would join Father Dichtl's missionary society, others would be encouraged to do so too.

As an essential preparation for missionary life, John tried under all circumstances to increase his love of God. On one occasion, he wrote in his journal, "My God, Thy hand lay heavily upon me today! Shame, sadness and vexation were mine. My cassock came home but it did not fit around the neck. The students all laughed at me. My neck was the source of greater vexation to me today than my sore throat some time ago.

But I thank Thee, O my Jesus, for this opportunity to mortify my vanity!"

To John's great disappointment, rumor was spread that Adalbert Schmidt had decided to join the Collegiate Society of Hohenfuhrt, an order of priests in Bohemia. Before long, word came from Adalbert that this was not true, but somehow, John felt a weakening of his resolve. Anton, he knew, had never wholly committed himself to being a missionary, but he had counted on Adalbert.

Just before graduation, several government officials visited the seminary. They were searching for a young priest with a knowledge of languages to take a position as foreign secretary in the government. This was a post that would have been coveted by many of the students, if they had the qualifications. They were forced to admit, however, that John was the only one able to fill it. He now could speak in German, Czech, Italian, French, English and Greek, as well as Latin and Hebrew. As gently as he could, he told these prominent men that he had other reasons behind his hard work, and that he could not take the position. Astounded, the men left the seminary. The president looked at John thoughtfully before he dismissed him with a nod.

At last graduation time rolled around. To their great chagrin, John and Anton learned that all were to be ordained except those from Budweis. They would have to return and take the canonical examination for the priesthood with the students in the town. His marks from Prague were outstanding, except for Moral Conduct, which to his great sorrow was "Fair."

His brother Wenzel and cousin Janson had come from Munich to represent the family at his ordination, only to find out that it had been deferred.

CHAPTER FOUR

TIME OF TRIAL

JOHN PASSED his second examination for the priesthood with the highest marks possible, but no date was set by the bishop of Budweis for ordination. It was deferred first because the old bishop was ill. On his recovery, the bishop delayed it again, as there were priests from the previous class that were unassigned. No one knew when John and his classmates would be ordained.

Word of the problem reached Prachatitz before John arrived home. For days his mother and sisters had spent much time at the window watching for him.

"Here he comes at last, Mother," exclaimed Joan from her post. Her mother and sisters ran to the window to watch John walk down the street towards them, his rucksack flung over his shoulder.

"My poor son," murmured his mother, half to to herself. "How discouraged you must feel." Then, wiping away a tear, she said, looking around, "All put on your most cheerful smile. We will have no crying." She flung open the door to receive him.

"Mother, mother," he said, taking her in his arms.

"John dear, this is a joyful day. You are home once again," she murmured as she kissed him.

Then it was the girls turn to hug him. They all gathered round chattering so fast that the dread moment of announcing failure never came. One of the girls ran to bring their father, and the circle was complete.

When there was a lull in the conversation, Mrs. Neumann said to John, "We all know that the bishop has delayed ordination, but it must be the will of God for some reason we can't see, so we will all have to be patient."

Once again, John was grateful for her understanding.

While gathering courage to tell his family of his missionary plans, John decided that he would visit shrines surrounding his home, of which there were many. Having sat at a desk for years, he gloried in the freedom to walk through the mountains and forests of Bohemia. Never one to lose sight of his main purpose, he also knew that he was strengthening himself both spiritually and physically for the ordeals he would face. The setbacks had not shaken his determination to go to America. "If I am not accepted as a priest," he thought, "I will find some place in America where I can be a hermit and pray for those who are in such need of help."

On February 14th he went to Budweis to meet Adalbert. Together they went to see Father Dichtl, who told them that through the rector at Strassburg he had received a request for two German priests to go to Philadelphia. He would recommend them, and apply to the Leopoldine Society for funds to send them. He would also request the episcopal consistory to apply for passports for them. All they had to do was to present themselves to the bishop and ask once again for ordination. If he still refused they were to ask for papers of permission to apply in another diocese for ordination.

"Here are the results of your examination for ordination. Present them to the bishop. They are the highest marks that can be given," he said to John.

Thanking him, and with high hopes of beginning their journey in a few weeks, John and Adalbert hurried to their appointment with the bishop. The eighty-year-old man was most gracious, but would not agree to an early ordination for the two budding missionaries. When they reminded him that they needed letters of permission, he said, "Yes, yes, you shall have them shortly."

"Now," said John, "I have the hardest task before me. I must not put off telling my family, since everything seems to be working well."

"Except our ordinations," said Adalbert.

"But, Father Dichtl counseled that we go without them if necessary."

"Somehow," said Adalbert, rubbing his chin with a nervous hand, "I do think I owe that to my family. They would want to share the joy with me."

"I do too, I do too, my friend," said John earnestly, "but it may be a year before the bishop consents to ordain us. Think of the time lost that never can be made up."

They parted with Adalbert's assurance that he would send for John when there was something else to be done.

As John tramped the fifteen miles to Prachatitz, he kept turning over in his mind the best way to break the news to his family. The opportunity came sooner that he expected. His father was at a meeting that evening and his mother and sisters sat around the living room in the dusk discussing the happenings of the day.

"And, I suppose, while in Budweis, you called on the bishop," teased his young sister Joan.

"As a matter of fact, I did," John replied, getting up to pace the room.

"Is something wrong, son?" asked his mother.

"Yes, and no," he replied, then realizing that was no answer at all, he blurted out, "For over three years I have been determined to go to America as a missionary." Glancing at the dumbstruck faces around him, he continued, "The bishop insists that he is delaying ordinations, but today he was willing for Adalbert and me to go."

"Without ordination?" gasped Veronica. "And then we would never see you as a priest, nor receive your blessing," she sobbed.

His mother had sat quietly through his announcement. Now she said, "When do you plan to go, John?"

"As soon as my papers are cleared."

In distress he insisted, "I must go, Mother. This, I know, is what God wants me to do."

She nodded. "All your life you have been taught to do the will of God as you saw it, and so now you must make the decision."

"I know, Mother."

"But, dear son," she continued, "have you thought well of the loneliness you will meet in that strange and fearful country? Have you considered the hardships and possible death? Can you bear separation from all you hold dear? Think well, John. If you can say 'yes' to my questions, then you must go."

"For three years, I have thought of nothing else," said John.

"Then it is settled. Now, girls, I don't want you to disturb John with any objections."

But privately, each sister in turn offered reasons why he should stay, the main one being that he would probably never see any of them again.

"Tell your father, John," his mother repeated to him each day for five days. On the sixth day, she made sure that the two had a chance to be alone.

Philip Neumann looked at his son in disbelief when he broke the news to him. After the first gasp, he tried to smile. "You certainly know how to keep secrets. If this is what you feel you should do, I will not put any barriers in your way. When do you go?"

"I will know tomorrow. Adalbert has written to me to come to Budweis to meet with the bishop. I hope it is good news."

"You have my blessing," said his father. Shaking his head, he added, "You have always been full of surprises, but this is the biggest of them all."

As he rose to walk to the door with his son, he laid his hand on the young man's shoulder. John noticed that it shook.

While he trudged to town, John kept thinking of his parents and prayed that he might have a small portion of their courage and faith.

On the 26th of July, John and Adalbert went again to see the bishop. In the week's interval he had changed his mind and was unwilling to let two such fine young men leave his diocese. Even so, he would not ordain them.

The Episcopal Consistory backed up the bishop. "Why are we educating you young men? You think you pay your own way, but you are an expense to the diocese. We cannot afford to have our young people running off," said one old priest.

"But my father, too, has invested heavily in my education, yet he is willing to give me to the service of God in America."

"That brings up another point," said a priest almost as old as the bishop. "Before we come to a decision, we must have your father's consent in writing."

"You won't take my word for it?" asked John.

"It is the regulation."

"Then you shall have it, sir."

Looking over his glasses, another member of the consistory said, "You can't leave now any-

way. Your passports have been held up on a
technicality."

John was aghast. He could not utter one word.
This time it was Adalbert who protested. "We
filled out all the forms sent to us."

"Just some minor point, I am sure," he was
told. "In a month, or two, three at the most, it
will be straightened out. You know how slow
those government agencies are. But remember,
we can do nothing without that note of consent."

"You shall have it tomorrow," promised John
grimly.

"Very well." They were dismissed with a nod.

Almost in despair, the two young men went to
see Father Dichtl. When they finished recounting
all the obstacles put in their path by the bishop
and his advisors, the priest looked at them gravely.
"I have another disappointment to add to your
litany of troubles."

"And that is . . . ?" asked John, feeling he
could not take much more.

"The Leopoldine Society feels that the request
for funds must come from the bishop of Philadelphia, not you. They will not send you to
America."

They both fumed. "Do they think that messages
fly? Has anyone informed Bishop Kenrick of this
breach of protocol?" Father Dichtl sat calmly
and watched the two dejected young men as they
vented their anger on the rules of the Society.
Then he said, "Now come on, you two. You will
never make good missionaries if you give in to
discouragement. Nothing ever seems to go right

for a missionary. That goes with the life you have chosen."

"But," protested John. "We are wasting too much valuable time."

"No, this is your period of trial. If you cannot accept opposition now, will you be able to do so in the missions? Learn, my good friends, to put yourselves in God's hands and go where He wills."

They had to agree that Father Dichtl was right. They would go home to wait, but they could also pray. And John would have the note from his father in the bishop's hands the next day. He could do that much.

Philip Neumann wrote the note giving John permission to become a missionary in America. As John was taking it to Budweis the next morning, his father walked by his side for some distance for he had business in a town which lay on the way. Walking together in the freedom of the mountains they found that they could talk more intimately, and John told his father all his plans and how they seemed to be coming to naught.

His father counseled that he leave the problem of his going to Father Dichtl and Adalbert, both of whom were in Budweis and could keep abreast of events.

John thought that wise advice, so he delivered to the bishop his note authenticated by the dean, and started for home. That 27th of July was hot and oppressive with sudden thunder storms coming over the mountains. It was after midnight when, wet and bedraggled, he reached home. Everyone was in bed asleep, but he found an unlocked kitchen window and climbed in. Great was the astonishment the next morning when he opened his door to join in family prayers.

Before long it was known throughout town that John intended to go to America. It was unheard of! In the opinion of many he would be wasting his talents and all the money his parents had spent on his education. To a friend who persisted in this vein, he put a question: "Why do you ship your goods to foreign markets?"

His friend gave the obvious reply, "Because in foreign markets, they command a higher price."

Looking at him steadily, John said, "For the same reason I want to go to America."

One by one, John silenced his critics, but all waited and watched for the day when he would reach America and find out for himself the awful situation there.

While waiting, John continued to walk to the many surrounding shrines. One day he visited Father Dichtl's brother who was pastor of a small church. He asked John to preach. It was the feast of the Nativity of the Blessed Virgin. When the young man returned home, his mother asked him how well he had preached.

"My sermon was not as successful as I hoped it would be, but I bore my failure with passable resignation." he said.

"John, stop teasing. I am sure it was fine Were many there?"

"The church was full. No doubt curiosity attracted many." As usual he refused to take credit for any success.

One night in December he was awakened by a bright light in his room. Realizing it was caused by a fire in a neighboring village made up of all wooden houses, he threw on some clothes, then paused at his father's door to alert him, before rushing off to help. When he arrived, the villagers were standing around helplessly. Calling for a ladder, he created a bucket brigade and climbed the ladder to dash water on the flames. He managed to contain the fire until help arrived. During the process he received a deep burn on his hand that was long in healing.

Finally, a letter came from Adalbert that the passports had arrived. He now could go to America. When he had first told his father of his intentions, Mr. Neumann had said, "If you believe yourself called by God, we shall put no obstacle in your way, but you must not take leave of us. We could not bear it."

So, knowing it was time to go, he called Veronica to his room, and insisting that she keep silent, told her he would leave in the morning. Then he announced that the next day he was going to Budweis. As he often went to the city, no one suspected he would not return. He packed few things to take with him, mostly books.

CHAPTER FIVE

TRAVEL TO AMERICA

AT DAWN the following day he set out out for Budweis. There he would catch the coach to begin the first leg of his journey to the new world. He knew now that he must go, but the way would be difficult. He had no money, and he was determined not to ask his parents to help him. They had done more than their share.

After a long tramp across the mountains, he came to the city which he now knew as well as his own town of Prachatitz. Adalbert Schmidt met him with good news — of sorts. Passports had been received, but they were good for only three years.

"Father Dichtl has been working hard on our behalf. He has found a mission society which will give us some money, and many of the priests interested in us have taken up a collection."

"How much in all do we have?" asked John.

"Two hundred francs.* It is not enough for two to go."

* About $40.00 in U.S. money.

With a sinking heart, John looked closely at his friend. "And you have decided not to go?"

"Not definitely, John, but I think it might be better to wait a while. One day I think I should go, the next day, I think better of it."

"In that case, you should wait. You must be certain. I am so determined to go to America that no one can stop me. And I think I've heard all the reasons. They are all prudent, but I will be happy to hear the last of them."

Smiling at John's vehemence, Adalbert said, "You must accept the money. I will give you no argument. Will you see the bishop again?"

"Of course," said John. "He is still my bishop, and I do want him to sign those papers."

When John called on the bishop, the old man, fearful of what lay ahead for a missionary, tried to dissuade him.

"If you have patience, you will be able to teach Scripture in the seminary. I hear you are a Bible scholar. Or," he added, "that post in the palace that you so rashly turned down, is still open. Are you sure you would not like that? You could do a great deal of good there."

"No, your Grace, I must go to America."

"Stubborn young man," muttered the bishop. "Go, if you must."

"But, my permission, sir?" asked John.

"Oh, that is right. I'll send it after you. Now I'll give you my blessing and you be on your way."

Adalbert was waiting outside the bishop's home. When he saw how dejected John looked, he thought the bishop had not been kind.

"I am going to travel with you today," he said.

"Thank you," said John. "But before I leave I must write to my parents. You will see that my letter is posted?"

"Of course," replied Adalbert.

Sitting in Adalbert's room, he wrote:

Dearest parents:

By my sudden and unexpected departure, I have tried to lessen the mutual pain of separating from you, as much on my account as on yours. Convinced that your parental blessing will accompany me wherever I go, I did not ask it of you before leaving for the reason above stated. . . . The career on which I am now about to embark, and which with God's help, I shall faithfully pursue, I am persuaded will bring spiritual blessing on you both.

At last it was time to board the coach for Linz. As they climbed in, Adalbert patted his friend on the shoulder. John gave him a wan smile. He was grateful for the companionship of his friend, though they had little to say. As they sat side by side, one thought of a boyhood dream that was dying, and the other of the loneliness and hardships he would face, and wondered how he would fare without the support of his friend.

The coach for Linz traveled through forests where the hard packed snow was fifteen feet deep. John looked at his beloved mountains and forests, and said good-bye to them too.

As they neared the town where they would part, John said, "The bishop tried to dissuade me. He said the letter would follow, and he did give me his blessing, so I know in the end he did not disown me. But without the letter who will ordain me?"

"Did he absolutely refuse permission?"

"No, he said he would send it after me."

Adalbert rubbed his chin thoughtfully. "He is getting old and forgetful. We must think of some kind friend who can remind him to send it."

"It would take him such a short time, and my problems would be less if I had it."

Adalbert looked at John closely. "Who said you would have no problems in this life you have chosen?"

A bit startled, John agreed. "I'll have to accept it. Maybe God doesn't want me to be a priest. The bishop may have good reason to distrust me."

"Oh no!" replied Adalbert. "He is just old and forgetful."

The coach bumped to a stop before the inn at Einsiedeln.

"This is where I must leave you, John," said Adalbert as they both alighted before the inn. Not bearing to prolong the leave-taking, and with both begging the other to pray for him, they gave each other a swift hug and Adalbert struck off down the road. With great sadness, John watched his retreating back. His last link with those he loved was severed.

The coach carried John on to Linz. There he called on the bishop, who invited him to dinner. The bishop was pleased that a young man wanted to take up such hard work. In those days America was mostly wilderness and tales of great hardship were told by returning missionaries. Explorers had barely reached the Pacific Ocean, and there were stories of high mountains. Mountains! John would be happy if he could live among them. At least one-third of the new country was not settled, and the villages were surrounded by great tracts of wilderness.

"If you are in need, I will see that you get help," said the bishop as they sat around the bountiful dinner table.

John thanked him, knowing the bishop could have influence with the Leopoldine Society. He also smiled ruefully to himself at the thought of his slender purse, and knew that a few francs more would ease his journey.

John's next stop was Munich. On arriving there, he went to the lodgings of his cousin Philip Janson, who was not at home. After searching the town for several hours, John came across his cousin as he was leaving the palace after a parade of the Royal Guards, of which he was a member. "How handsome you look," said John, admiring his cousin in his fine uniform touched with gold braid. Then, glancing down at his own suit, which was showing signs of wear, he added, "The army I am trying to join doesn't have such splendid outfits. If they did, I would look very silly in them."

Philip was anxious to hear how his cousin had fared in the last six months. He was indignant at the treatment John had received, and said so.

"Oh, no, Philip, I am afraid that they found

some grave defect in me, or the letters would have been given to me at home."

"How I wish I could go with you!" exclaimed his cousin. "You will have many exciting experiences."

"But, Philip, I am not doing it for fun, I am very sure there will be very little of that."

Later Philip went back on duty, and John, following the roads pointed out to him, came to the seminary to which he had letters of introduction. The rector was away, but John was welcomed. There he met Father Henni, a German missionary recently returned from America. He had labored on the frontiers, and later became bishop of Milwaukee. Full of questions, John told this older man of his hopes.

The priest looked at the eager young man through tired eyes. "You say you hope to go to Philadelphia to help the Germans there."

"Yes."

"You are not needed there," he said abruptly.

"No? but I thought—"

"Listen to me, young man," the priest interrupted. "Philadelphia does not like Catholics. I have never visited there myself, but I am told that the Germans living there are a troublesome lot. They will not listen to a young boy like you; moreover, most of them have pushed out into the wilderness. They have huddled together ten or twenty families at a crossroads. Did I say crossroads? I mean where two trails cross one another. They are not roads. These people have

to cut out roads in the wilderness for themselves.
I know. I have ridden them both on horseback
and by wagon. They are not comfortable like
our stages."

John thought back on the last few days, and
how tired he was after a day's journey on well-
kept roads. He rubbed his back as if to take out
the kinks and privately resolved to trust to his
own two legs for as much traveling as he would
have to do.

"If you must go, go farther west. You might
find someone who needs you."

"But—"

"And," continued the priest, "these people
are rough, strong, big people who will look down
on a frail boy like you."

"I have great endurance, and am not young.
When I receive my permission, I can be ordained
a priest. A priest, no matter how short, brings
Christ to His people," John protested.

The priest sat up straight. "No letter of permission! No one will have you. You are wasting
your time. Stay home, boy, stay home!"

John was greatly cast down by Father Henni's
advice. Discouraged, he went to his room, then
to church where he prayed a long time for guidance. He then decided that he would go to Paris.
Bishop Bruté of Vincennes, Indiana was expected
there shortly. Since Philadelphia no longer needed
him, possibly he could find a post in Vincennes.

While still in Munich, he stopped at a mission
society in the hope of receiving some financial
aid. None was forthcoming, but he was loaded

down with pamphlets and books that the society thought might be useful in the new world. It did not occur to them that as he often traveled by foot, he would have to carry the books or send them by coach. The cost of freight would have to come out of his slender means. He wrote in his diary that, "Out of my poor purse, I have to pay freight on other people's books." But then, he added that if they would be of use to someone, the meals he had to lose to pay for them were worth it.

All during his trip through Europe, he was given advice, much of it bad. When he reached Strassburg, Canon Rass of the seminary there, who had forwarded the word of the need in Philadelphia, told John that the need had been fulfilled, and that the money which he was to receive there had been given to another.

"You could try Bishop Bruté of Vincennes, Indiana, who is in Paris, or you could go to New York. I will write Bishop Dubois and tell him you are coming to America." He also gave him a number of books, which again had to be transported at John's expense. The canon seemed cold and indifferent.

Nevertheless, John thanked him and hurried to catch the coach for Nancy. There he met Father Schaefer, who was going to Vincennes and was to meet Bishop Bruté in Paris. They traveled together to Paris, and after some trouble were able to find cheap lodgings with the Foreign Mission Society there.

John found Paris shocking. Many people there

were in carnival dress, yet churches were thronged. During the time he waited for the bishop, he visited churches and browsed through bookstores. In spite of his dwindling funds, he found books that he longed to own. Having bought a few, he decided that the only way he could stop spending all his money was to stay in his room when he was not in church.

Thus a month passed in Paris, and still no word from the bishop as to the date of his return. Maybe he had not received John's request to join those working in Vincennes. His hopes for working in Vincennes dimming, John decided to go to New York.

On Easter, he counted up his remaining resources. If he did not start at once, he would not have enough to pay his passage. So, he engaged a seat on a coach for the port of Le Havre, from which he could get a ship for New York.

Arriving at the appointed time, he found that the coach for which he had paid twenty-nine of his precious francs to transport him and his books, had left five minutes earlier. He hired a cab hoping to overtake it, but not doing so at the city gates, he decided to walk. After walking all night in the drenching rain, he caught up with the coach the next morning when it stopped at Nantere. From then on, knowing that he did not have enough money to stay the night in inns, he walked by day and at nightfall he waited for the next coach. At one stop all the passengers got off to dine. John, tired, and hungry and with a headache, thought he could not afford the price of dinner and walked up and down before the inn. The innkeeper's wife called him.

"Come in here and have some dinner."

"But, madam, a slice of bread would be fine. I do not have the funds for a large meal."

"Eat, eat," she said. "We will not quarrel about the bill."

When John had eaten his fill, he thanked her for her great kindness. She smiled in reply and said, "Pray for us!"

John climbed to his perch beside the driver, wondering at the goodness of God to supply him in his need.

At last they arrived at Le Havre. Here, John discovered that, in spite of his studies, he needed much more practice in both French and English. He had to be very careful so that no one would take advantage of him. After he stopped in a church to thank God for his safe arrival, John went to look at the harbor. The sight of such a great expanse of water almost overwhelmed the mountain boy. Among the ships lying at the quay was the *Europa*. It was a large ship, a three-master, and seemed built to withstand storms. The captain haggled with him, and finally agreed to take him to America for eighty francs. This was passage only. For seven francs, he bought a straw mattress and pillow, and for fifty francs, he arranged with the steward to lay in some food for him. Thus, ready, he paid his innkeeper and climbed aboard. In his pocket was a five franc note, just one dollar in American money.

To make as much money as possible, the captain crowded as many as he could on the lower decks. Scarcely could anyone find room to spread his mattress. The immigrants were unfriendly. Many jeered when John said his prayers.

It was worse when he tried to write in his diary in his native German. "What are you writing?" one man asked, and tried to peer over his shoulder. "A letter to your sweetheart?"

John ignored him, but from that time on he wrote his diary in French instead of German.

The voyage to America took forty days. Two years later, steamships made a regular passage in ten days, but the cost was far beyond the means of immigrants for some time.

Fortunately, John quickly became accustomed to the sea and suffered rarely from seasickness. There were four long days of violent storm which threatened to blow them back to port. In one of those gales, John was standing on the deck lost in thought about his future. Suddenly he felt himself pushed forward as by an invisible hand. The sailyard came crashing down on the spot he had just vacated. From that moment on, he knew he was in the hands of God.

At last seaweed could be seen floating by the ship. Land could not be far away. Finally the glad sound rang out: "Land Ho!"

In spite of the rain that drenched them that day, passengers lined the deck until night fell. What wonderful sights. Green grass, tall trees, and neat cottages could be seen from the ship. The immigrants shouted with joy and began to gather their belongings together. The captain soon checked their exuberance with his announcement that they would not go ashore for several days. He wanted the sick to recover before he took them to be checked by the immigration authorities.

John was so anxious to land that six times he went to the captain to ask if he could be put ashore on Staten Island.

When the captain saw him coming for the seventh time, he shouted to his mate. "Get someone to row this man to the island. I am sick of him." So off John went to Staten Island. He arrived in America with a dollar in his pocket, and no hat, as someone had stolen it aboard ship. His shoes were worn out and his coat almost threadbare, but he was in America and ready to begin his mission. For a few cents the sidewheeler *Hercules* brought him to the Battery on Manhattan Island. From there he started to search for a Catholic church.

CHAPTER SIX

A MISSIONARY

IN THE FIFTY YEARS since the defeated British had sailed from New York harbor, the city had mushroomed. During the 1830's, half a million immigrants arrived in America, and a great many of them came to New York City. John Neumann, even though he had prayed and thought about nothing else except coming to this new country, really had no idea of what it was like.

When he landed on Manhattan Island at one o'clock in the afternoon on the feast of Corpus Christi, his first thought was to find a church to thank God for his safe arrival. In the pouring rain, with his bag clutched in his hand, he trudged down one street and up another looking for a church. In Bohemia, every few blocks there was a church surmounted by a cross. When he looked to the sky for a familiar steeple, he did see a few. Hurrying towards one, he realized that it was topped by a weather vane. That could not be the church he was looking for. A man in uniform was walking along the street swinging a club.

Stopping before him, John asked, "Please sir, direct me to a Catholic church."

The policeman scratched his head, trying to understand John's English and finally said, "Oh, a church! I see! Go around this corner."

Reaching a building that looked like a meeting hall, and with no steeple at all, John found the doors locked. Peering at the nameplate, he read, "First United Church." What was that? At least he knew that it was not the one he sought. Then he found Holy Trinity Church and saw that it was Episcopalian.

This was a strange city. There were no ancient buildings as in Prague, or even in Prachatitz. No walls surrounded it. It was not crowded, as were European cities. It was spread out with grass in many areas and massive trees shading the streets, more like a village. Some of the streets were paved with rough cobblestone and some were merely hard packed dirt. Street vendors hawked water and fruits. Their cries could be heard everywhere. The poor people he passed were often in their national costume and spoke in many languages. Carriages constantly clattered past, carrying ladies in silks and satins. This country was called a democracy, but some dressed like kings. The coachmen were a source of wonder. They all had shiny black skin. John had never seen black men before. They must be Africans. He had heard of America importing slaves and was shocked. Imagine enslaving another soul! When he saw these people for the first time he prayed for them.

John wandered the streets of New York for five hours looking for a church with a cross over it. He had great difficulty in making people understand his English, and resolved that as soon as possible, he would learn correct pronounciation.

Finally, he came to a tavern and read on it the name of the owner. It sounded German. He stopped to inquire. The innkeeper, a Swiss, gave him a meal and lodging for the night.

"In the morning," he said, "I will direct you to a Catholic church."

That evening, John sat in the public room trying to accustom his ears to hearing the English language. Indeed, he heard English spoken, but he also heard French, Italian and German, along with a smattering of what he decided must be Gaelic.

True to his word, the next morning, after John had settled his bill and looked ruefully at the few pennies he had left, the innkeeper gave him directions.

"Walk down three blocks and turn to your left. There you will find a small church recently bought from the Protestants. It is called Christ Church."

Following directions, he came to a tiny church. With a feeling of disbelief that he had finally reached his goal, he pushed open the door and found himself in familiar surroundings. He was not away from home at all. After praying for some time, he left the church and knocked on the door of the priest's house. There he met Father Schneller, who was most friendly and gave him the address of the bishop's home. As he was giving John the directions, he said, "The only German priest we have in New York is Father John Raffeiner. He happens to live with the bishop. You can kill two birds with one stone." Father Schneller opened the door and pointed the direction to John.

Thanking him, John started on his way. "Kill two birds," he pondered. He did not want to kill anything, much less the birds who were singing joyously that bright June morning. Finally, John realized he would have to wait until he could get someone to explain the priest's remark. There was so much to learn in America.

Before long, he reached the bishop's door and asked for Father Raffeiner. When he had introduced himself, the good priest greeted him warmly, but with a look of astonishment. "How did you get here?" was his first question.

Mystified, John explained that he had come on the *Europa,* which was probably still lying off Staten Island.

"But it was only three weeks ago that Bishop Dubois, having heard from Canon Rass, wrote accepting you and two other seminarians into his diocese. The angels must have carried you."

As he thought back on his travels, John decided that if they had, they had given him a bumpy trip.

"We must not sit here talking," said Father Raffeiner. He rose and hurried John to the door. "The bishop must be told of your arrival." Going across the hall, they found Bishop Dubois busy

in his office. Without any preliminary, Father
Raffeiner said, "Your Grace, here is John
Neumann, our German seminarian." John knelt
to kiss the bishop's ring.

"Welcome," said the kindly bishop as he helped
John to rise. "Come, sit down and tell us how you
have been able to reach here so soon." He in-
dicated seats for his visitors and sat quietly behind
his desk. A veteran missionary, Bishop Dubois
had been the advisor of Elizabeth Seton in
Emmitsburg, and although now over seventy, gave
all his time and strength to this sprawling diocese.

The story of John's great desire to be a missionary and all the blocks put in his way, did not
take long in the telling. Little chirps of sympathy
came from the bishop. Then came the forlorn
part.

"The letter of permission from the bishop of
Budweis has not reached me. I am afraid I can't
be the help I had hoped to be."

"Nonsense," said the bishop who knew the
great needs of the missionary country. "That
letter is on its way, I am sure, and is held up
some place, possibly in the hold of a ship. You
have all your other papers showing you are ready
for ordination. We can't let one letter stop God's
work. I will ordain you tomorrow."

"Your Grace," gasped John. "I am not prepared. Life on shipboard left me very little opportunity for prayer."

"A few days of recollection would be good,"
agreed the bishop. "Tomorrow I go for a visit to
some of the churches, but will be back in three
weeks, and then I will ordain you."

Reaching into a drawer he took out some money. "In the meantime, do get a new suit and a pair of shoes. I can't have my priests walking the streets of New York barefoot. How much money do you have?"

John put his hand into his pocket and brought out the few coins left.

Bishop Dubois looked at them, then at the young man. He put his hand in the drawer again, and came out with a gold piece. "Father Raffeiner, do take care of this young man and see he also gets a cassock before he gives this away. I suppose you do have a cassock of sorts?" he asked, looking at John.

"The only one I have fits me ill. I will have to grow around the neck."

The bishop laughed, "I can see you will be a problem to me. But I like the kind of problems you'll create." With a pat on the back and his blessing, he dismissed the young man.

Dazed, John left the bishop's house and went to Saint Nicholas Church with Father Raffeiner. He fully expected to spend the few weeks in prayer and instruction, as was customary in Budweis. In Europe, anyone preparing for ordination spent some weeks in a special retreat with his director, preparing himself for the great sacrament. But Father Raffeiner had so much to do that he could spare little time for John. Instead, he turned over to him a class of thirty pupils to instruct for their first Holy Communion. John was happy to help these children prepare for their special day, yet he felt a little sad that he did not have much direction in his own preparations.

Less than a month later, he was ordained without the friends and celebration he would have had at home, but he was satisfied, even though he greatly missed the joy of having his family with him. The next day many parishioners came to his first Mass, and he had the pleasure of giving Holy Communion to his class of thirty. Afterwards they all crowded around him to express their love for him.

As soon as Father Raffeiner had met John, he had pleaded with the bishop to let the young priest stay in New York City to help with all the German immigrants pouring into that port. Bishop Dubois could not yield to the pleas of Father Raffeiner. It was with deep regret that he refused the request.

"I know that several thousand Germans land in New York every month, but most of them settle in the upper part of the state. It is then that they most need our help. The situation is desperate here, but in that 900-square-mile parish of Buffalo, there is only one German speaking priest. He must have help. How I wish others had come with this young man! But we must be content with what God sends us."

So, three days after his ordination, Father John Neumann, resplendent and feeling somewhat foolish in a suit, shoes and hat of American cut, stepped on to the steamboat which would take him to Albany. He was impressed with the vastness of this new country. In little Budweis there were too many priests, but in the whole diocese of New York with its 200,000 Catholics there were only thirty-six priests, thirty-one of them

Irish, and only three German, four, now that he,
unbelievable as it sounded, was ordained. He
recalled how half the congregation could not get
into the church the previous Sunday, but clustered
around the door and windows in an effort to
participate in the Mass.

Although it took twelve hours to make the
journey to Albany Father Neumann was excited
by the sights and sounds around him. The ship
first passed large estates that back home would
have been owned by royalty. These faded into
vast expanses of forests. Occasionally, he saw a
deer or even a bear coming to the river to drink.
Birds were everywhere. Scattered along the river
in little clearings were huddled clusters of huts.
The people living in such communities were those
to whom he was expected to minister. John
prayed that he could be of help to them.

Finally he arrived in Albany. With letters of
introduction in hand, he made his way to the
Church of Saint Mary. He spent the night with
the priest and said Mass alone for the first time.

That morning John took the steam train to
Schenectady, a city whose name he found very
difficult to pronounce. He recalled the horsedrawn
railroad of Budweis, but this was different. The
Mohawk and Hudson Railroad, completed between Schenectady and Albany only five years
earlier, was one of the wonders of the day.

But to the young priest, the part that made it
impressive was that it traveled at the incredible
speed of ten miles an hour without running off
its track. Unfortunately, its run was short. At
Schenectady, covered with soot and grime, he

transferred to a canal boat that would take him to Rochester at the rate of four miles an hour.

During the four days of leisurely travel, the barge master, proud of his work, told the newcomer about the canals and how they had been a great factor in linking villages and towns.

"This barge can haul as much freight with the help of a team of horses, as can be drawn over the highways in one hundred wagons," he boasted.

There was one thing sure, thought John, it may not be a faster mode of travel, but it was much more pleasant. For miles, he would walk along the tow path, marvelling at the plants and flowers he saw on the way. He began to collect American specimens and make notes to send back to all his botantist friends in Budweis.

As the barge neared Rochester, all could hear shouts and fireworks. When Father Bernard O'Reilly, who was standing on the landing waiting for his visitor, saw the look of puzzlement on John's face, he laughed.

"Sorry to say," he said, after greeting the new priest, "all this excitement is not for you. It is the Fourth of July, the day America celebrates its independence. But you are indeed welcome in Rochester."

This frontier town was different from anything that Father Neumann had ever seen. Everyone seemed to be doing something different, and doing it out loud. There were great shouts at impromptu horse races down the road. Children were romping, and many men were drunk.

"You are in the country, where only the hardy ones come. They live hard lives, and play hard," said Father O'Reilly. "You will get used to their rough manners."

Once back at his small house, the priest explained that when he had been sent to Rochester, the population was mostly Catholic Irish. With work on the canals and railroads, other nationalities had come into the town. These people were mostly German speaking, a good number of them Catholic. "Unfortunately, I do not know their language, and they cannot understand mine. A Redemptorist, Father Prost, stopped here last year, and now has been assigned to this area. Bishop Dubois sent you to fill in for a few days until the new pastor's arrival."

"I understand my stay here will be brief."

"Let me warn you, however, these people have built their own church, and I fear will want to govern it themselves."

When Father Neumann met the trustees, as they called the leading men of the parish, he realized that the warning he had received was only too true.

"You are too young to tell us that we sin," one man told him.

"It is not I who tell you, it is God speaking through me, and I do not think my youth matters," he replied.

They liked the way the young priest stood up to them, and grudgingly agreed that he might stay until the new pastor arrived.

Realizing that the future of the faith rested in the children, Father Neumann gathered them together to teach them their catechism. He found that they could speak scarcely any English, and that their German was very bad. With no one to teach them, they were growing like weeds, having little communication with their parents. Schools, he determined, were essential in the frontiers.

When the new pastor arrived, John spent a few days with him before continuing on to Buffalo. During that time, the new priest was greatly impressed by Father Prost's piety and devotion to the Redemptorist rule. To him the young man confided his uneasiness about not receiving the letter of permission from the bishop of Budweis.

"I am worried that the papers have not arrived and I feel that I am working in America unlawfully without them."

"Please do not let that bother you," advised Father Prost. "The urgent need of your services here is not understood in Europe. There is no doubt of the lawfulness of your ordination by Bishop Dubois."

Having always lived by the rule, Father Neumann had to be satisfied, but he could not keep from hoping the letter would arrive soon.

The next day, he took the barge along the canal to his mission in Buffalo. When he arrived at dusk, the lamplighter had finished lighting the kerosene lamps that dotted the unpaved streets. Although he walked to Lewis Street to the home of Father Pax, his new superior, he might have taken the car that was drawn by horses over rails, but he thought he would defer that pleasure for another day.

Father Pax, a young man, greeted John warmly. "I am most happy to see you," he said. "Maybe I will sleep better at nights, since I have someone to help care for the thousands that continue to pour into this area."

Buffalo had become a gateway to the west. Many had been drawn there by work on the canal, and had stayed. This heavily populated town was surrounded by a wilderness of forests, swamps and mountains. In this area there were pockets of settlements. John recalled that Father Henni in Munich had said that there were German settlements at the crossings of trails. When he told Father Pax of this remark, the young priest nodded in agreement. "So it seems. The hamlet of Williamsville has four families in it."

As they were discussing plans for helping the parish, Father Pax said, "I think it would be wiser to divide our efforts. Would you prefer to work in the city or the surrounding country?"

Always eager to assume the heavier burden, Father Neumann replied, "I am a country boy and will work well in the outlying churches."

Father Pax thought it best for the new priest to make his headquarters at Williamsville. True, it boasted of a stone church, but money had run out and there was no roof, nor windows, and the floor was dirt. A temporary altar and a few crude benches were all the furnishing. The church, which had been so ambitiously begun several years previously, had never been finished because some who had promised to donate time now wanted to be paid. After studying the situation, Father Neumann succeeded in settling the problems. He then had to deal with some unfriendly youths who thought it great fun to disrupt services.

When Father Neumann took over the parish he was delighted to learn there was a school attached. One day he visited the school unexpectedly and found the schoolmaster drunk, and abusing one of the children.

"Take your hat, go home and do not return," he said sternly.

All watched the teacher until he was out of sight, then one of the children said, "Sir, who will teach us now?"

"I will," said their pastor. "Who will begin to read?" Since he was an expert in mathematics, knew botany better than most, and had studied history, Father Neumann gave the children a good education in secular as well as religious subjects.

Even though he was teaching school, he tramped long distances to the other churches, sometimes as many as forty miles. The country was suffering a money crisis, and the promised yearly salary of $300 was never given to the priest. In fact, he received little or nothing. Shrugging his shoulders, he would say, "If you want to be a missionary, you must love poverty."

The farmers, seeing how far their priest walked, gave him a horse. Possibly aware that the little man knew nothing about horses and how to ride them, the animal tried in every way he could to unseat his master — and often did. Until they got to know one another better, Father Neumann took to leading the horse, which he loaded with his Mass kit and vestments. Often the days that he had teased Adalbert about riding in the missions came to John's mind, and he laughed at himself. "I wish Adalbert were here to tame this animal." In time the horse did allow his master to mount and they ambled through forest trails together.

From Williamsville, Father Neumann moved to North Bush. He had to board with a family who lived a mile and a half from the little log church. Each day, in all kinds of weather, he walked to the church early in the morning through the swampy forest. Finally the parishioners erected a tiny two-room cabin beside the church to house their priest. He furnished it with four chairs and two trunks. He slept on the dirt floor. Often he ate cold meals or skipped them altogether. The women, when they did not see any smoke coming from his fireplace, knew he was not cooking. Although very poor, and having little to eat themselves, they would offer him food when he came to see them. To avoid embarrassment, he made sure that he never visited a home at mealtime.

Besides the farm settlers, many rough mountain men were in the area. One day one of them challenged him with slurs on the church. Father Neumann turned to walk away.

"You, priest," yelled the man. "Answer me when I speak to you."

Father Neumann never turned around, but the bystanders who knew the temper of the man, were aghast.

"Hey, you priest," bellowed the man even louder, and whipped out his gun. "Answer me when I talk to you, or I'll shoot you dead."

Father Neumann hesitated a second, then continued on his way.

In disgust, the man threw down his gun. "Can't shoot a man in his back," he muttered.

Father Neumann worked himself to a point of exhaustion. One evening, returning from a forty-mile hike to an outpost, tired to the bone and his feet blistered, he sank against a tree. Oblivious of the mosquitos that swarmed around him he fell into a deep sleep. Suddenly he woke to see a circle of dark menacing faces around him. It was an Indian war party returning home. In fear, John blessed himself and started to pray. The chief stopped a warrior with a raised tomahawk. "Look, he is a black-robe. Do not harm him." Gently they placed him on a buffalo robe and carried him to the nearest farmhouse, then stole away as silently as they had come.

John wrote home regularly. Yet not once in three years did he hear directly from his family. While letters from others reached him, those from his parents did not. This was a source of worry to him. There were so many things to write about. He kept sending word of the crying need for help and urged that others be recruited to come to America as missionaries. His brother Wenzel, fired by his letters, begged permission of his parents to join John.

"You have read of the hardships your brother endures," said his father. "Do you think you can bear up under them?"

"I would like to try, father, and besides, John needs me."

His mother smiled. "That is the best answer you have given yet, my son, only you should have said, 'God and John need me!' "

Hugging his mother, Wenzel replied, "You know that is what I mean, Mother. I did put it badly."

So Wenzel came to America to live with John in his little log cabin. What great joy Wenzel brought. "I never thought I would see you again, dear brother, nor hear news directly from my family," he said.

"My passport has run out, and I have applied for American citizenship, so I am here to stay," added the priest.

With the arrival of his brother, Father Neumann's tasks became lighter. Wenzel became the schoolmaster and the builder who completed the churches. In his few spare moments, Father Neuman studied English and botany. He also studied about the medicinal properties of plants so that he could help his people in their physical illnesses. But most of all, Father Neumann had some time to give to prayer. He prayed often as he walked through the marshy forests to his many missions. One night he became confused and completely lost. Praying for help he saw a faint light. Following in that direction, he came to a hovel, and knocked on the door. A child's voice called to him. "Go away, we do not open our door after dark." Persisting, he finally persuaded the child to let him in. When he entered, he saw a man, seemingly dying, lying on a bed of moss, and a frightened child standing by. With some of

his altar wine he revived the man, who was
delighted to see a priest. Through the night,
Father Neumann nursed the man, who came
through the crisis. Later, he learned that the
mother and another child had died, and the father
and the little girl were all who were left.

Even though he was labouring hard to spread
the love of God and love of prayer, John felt
that he, himself was growing less fervent. This
worried him considerably.

The bishop asked Father Neumann if he would
go back to Rochester for a short time. The trustees
were making it difficult for the priest. Germans
at that time were used to the state paying the
expenses of the church, and felt no responsibility
for supporting it themselves. In America, where
they had to support their church or do without
one, the parishioners felt that they should have
the full right to order the priest to do anything
they wished. Since they could not order church
affairs, great disagreements arose. So, Father
Neumann went back to Rochester in 1838. With
his usual tact, he settled the trustee problem.
While there, he could not help but note that in
spite of the unruly trustees the parishioners had
grown in piety, and were much more fervent in
their prayers than they had been two years
previously. "This is due to the work of the
Redemptorists," he told his friend Father O'Reilly.

Back in his own area, he felt it necessary to
open several more missions. One of them was
near Niagara Falls. He wrote to his parents of
the falls. At home they had marvelled over a
steel engraving of them. "I am so near them that

I can hear the roar of the cataract in my room. It sounds like a distant hailstorm. I have not yet visited the falls." There is no record that he ever saw them.

In the four years of his parish work, Father Neumann was terribly lonely for the help and companionship of fellow priests. He saw Father Pax in Buffalo only occasionally. Finally he became ill from a combination of undulant fever, overwork and lack of nourishment. Wenzel nursed him carefully during the three months he was ill. In spite of his illness he insisted on saying Sunday Mass. But, strange as it may sound, although he had been constantly called out during the previous years to minister to his parishioners, not one sick call was received during his illness, so he did not feel that he was abandoning his people.

During these months he thought and prayed and decided that he could serve God better if he joined a community of priests. Having so admired the work of the Redemptorists, he wrote to Father Prost, now superior of the order in America, asking to be admitted to the order.

Bishop Hughes, successor to Bishop Dubois, who had retired in 1839, did not want to lose such a valuable worker, and refused to give Father Neumann permission to leave the diocese. Finally, he was persuaded to agree. At that time, Wenzel decided to follow in his brother's footsteps and join the Redemptorists too. Once more, John Neumann's life was taking an unexpected turn.

CHAPTER SEVEN

A HAVEN SOUGHT

AS IN ALL his other efforts, Father Neumann had to overcome great difficulties when he wanted to become a Redemptorist priest. He was not trying to run away from the hard work in his parishes, but he was not well.

"I find I am not that strong mountain boy I used to be. My recurring fever seems to have proved that," he told Father Pax. "However," he added, "I am still strong enough to do my duty. My purpose in this move is to strengthen myself in the love of God, so I will be better prepared to help others. Unless I have spiritual help myself, I will surely fail."

Having received his letter of acceptance from Father Prost on September 16, 1840, he wrote to Bishop Hughes requesting one or more priests as replacements for him in the churches surrounding Buffalo. The bishop was away visiting his parishes and did not receive Father Neumann's letter.

After waiting for three weeks, he decided to leave his problems in the hands of Father Prost and Father Pax and set off for Pittsburgh.

By October 13th, he was able to get passage

on a small ship headed for Erie, a ninety-mile overnight trip. The greedy captain overloaded the steamer so that there was standing room only. No one could sit or lie down, and no food was provided. It reminded Father Neumann of his trip to America. A fierce wind on the lake drove the ship back to Buffalo, where the captain refueled and started out again. Once more on its way, the ship was again caught up in the storm and driven off its course. The next morning found them in nearly the same spot as they had been the previous night. At last, the captain having borrowed coal from a passing steamer, the ship finally reached port at Erie. The trip had taken two full days.

Exhausted, Father Neumann rested for a few days with the priest in town, and then took the stagecoach for Pittsburgh, where he anticipated a year of quiet prayer and meditation in his novitiate for the Redemptorist order. He was disturbed that he had not yet received permission from Bishop Hughes to leave his diocese. He knew that dear old Bishop Dubois would have given it to him immediately, but the new bishop was reluctant to lose his help. He need not have worried this time, as his papers were in Pittsburgh waiting for him.

Eight years before John Neumann asked to join them, the Redemptorist order had sent three priests and three lay brothers to America. These men planned to establish an American foundation to fulfill their mission of preaching and giving missions to help Catholics to renew their fervor. Once in America, they found the situation so dire that they had to separate immediately and help as best they could where the need was most pressing. Since all spoke German, the demand for their help was great. Before long they were scattered, acting as pastors in far-flung areas. It was when Father Prost came to Rochester that John Neumann had his first contact with the American Redemptorists. John was greatly impressed with Father Prost's piety and his devotion to the rule of his order. These men knew that they had to have some headquarters or foundation where they could congregate, say their prayers together, and strengthen one another in their spiritual life. Finally, by April 1839, Father Prost bought a factory in Pittsburgh. Part of it was converted into a church and the other part into a foundation for the order. It was here that Father Neumann, the first American priest novice, went in the certainty that he would receive a year of religious instruction and of prayer.

Father Neumann was greeted with loving kindness by the superior, who said, "I know you are tired, but we are terribly short-handed here. I have assigned High Mass tomorrow to you. You will also preach."

From that day on, he was a member of the working team. The spiritual director assigned to him immediately went off on a mission. There were so few to do so much work.

Pittsburgh, a thriving industrial town at the meeting of two rivers, was heavily populated with Germans, who comprised ten percent of the fifty thousand citizens. Most of them were Catholic. This period in American history was called the "roaring 40's." Crises popped up constantly. How,

in this air of unrest, could John be quiet and
pray? He was almost in despair. All day, and even
into the night, he was busy with parish affairs.

In November, John welcomed his brother
Wenzel, who had decided to join the Redemptorists as a lay brother.

"My dear brother," said John, "I am so happy
to see you. Do not, however, think you have
found a haven such as the European monasteries."

"So I judged," answered Wenzel. "Where do
you go next?"

"Wherever I am sent. Our Lord was a wanderer
from place to place. Who am I to even hope that
it will be any different for me?"

The Redemptorists, seeing so much work to be
done, and no one else to do it, tried to do too
many things. They had missions in northern New
York, Pennsylvania, Ohio, and Maryland. Since
Father Neumann was a priest he was needed
badly, and his services were used at the expense
of his regular training in the rule of the Redemptorist order.

Immigrants were pouring into the country.
Only the more adventurous or the desperate dared
to take the hazardous journey across the Atlantic.
They could not afford passage on the new steam-
ers, and so had to endure the holds of the sailing
ships. The weaker died, and the bold survived.

America was expanding westward and north-
ward from the port cities. Hiring bosses were on
docks offering jobs to the poor as they arrived.
Many of these immigrants found themselves in
the wilderness working on railroads. Father
Neumann worried about these poor people. Yet,

from bitter experience, he know how badly needed was some form of transportation other than the stagecoach or horseback. Unlike Europe, the distances were so vast.

"I have had enough trouble with horses," he said to someone who urged that he travel by horse from mission to mission. "The stagecoach provides a special kind of penance, but until these marvelous railroads everyone talks about are completed, I must endure them."

The stagecoaches in America often were a sort of wagon with a plank across. As many as could be crowded in sat knee to knee enduring as best they could the jouncing they received as the horses plodded along the roads that often were overgrown with weeds and dotted with boulders.

When in May 1841, Father Neumann was sent to Saint John's Church in Baltimore, where another foundation was to be established with new recruits for the missions from Europe, he heaved a sigh of relief. At last there was to be time for recollection. Three days later, the superior called him. "I am sorry, Father," he said, "but I must send you to New York City."

Obediently, he packed his bag and went to New York. By mail two weeks later, he was directed to go to Rochester, where twice he had mediated with the trustees. Once more he began to establish good relations with the parishioners, only to be whisked off to Buffalo. But this assignment was a pleasure. Father Pax had become ill and Father Neumann was happy to spend six weeks helping his friend. While he was busy all day with the affairs of the parish, at night the two friends could spend a few hours together.

"I have been a novice for almost a year now, and have had no constant instruction. My days seem to be spent in trying to catch up with my novice-master," said Father Neumann while he sat by his friend's bed one evening.

"Maybe, for this country, one needs a different kind of novitiate," suggested Father Pax.

"I am having that," replied Father Neumann ruefully. "Sometimes I wonder if I made the right decision." Recovering, Father Pax was able to work once more, and orders came for Father Neumann to go to Norwalk, Ohio where his novice-master was at the moment.

Sadly, Father Neumann said, "I should never have joined the Redemptorists. Here I am flying from one church to another, never staying long enough to be of any use."

"All America is in turmoil. How can you expect in times like these that your religious order pull back into its shell?" Father Pax asked.

"I know that I am being unreasonable, but I do long for some spiritual help and companionship. I know I can get it from the men in my order if things ever settle down," John replied.

While in Buffalo, John wrote to his friend, Father Prost.

"Since the superiors are sending me from pillar to post, I have the thought that maybe they do not want me."

Father Prost replied immediately saying that "There has never been a single order in which no fault occurred. The present problem comes from trying to do too many things. Go to Norwalk. It is better that money be spent in traveling than to be disobedient."

In Norwalk, Ohio, while once again with his novice-master, each spent so much time in traveling to help scattered parishioners that John received very little assistance.

At last, the superior realized that he had driven his novice too hard, and that he had thoughts of leaving the order. So he sent directions for Father Neumann to return to Baltimore, but by easy stages. He was to give missions on the way.

By now John Neumann could not look at a stagecoach without shuddering. The one he had to ride to Canton in mid-November was open, and the passengers huddled together in the pouring rain without any means of shelter.

Once in Canton, at the priest's house, he met the bishop of Cincinnati and his vicar-general, who was none other than Father Henni, who had offered such discouraging advice in Munich.

Still gloomy, he told Father Neumann that he had heard that the American Redemptorists were about to disband, and that was why they had no regular novitiate.

"Come with us to Cincinnati," urged the bishop. "I will give you a parish."

Thanking them, Father Neumann decided he would wait a while. But he could scarcely bide his time until he reached Baltimore. There he saw that work was progressing on Saint Alphonsus Church. The order surely would not begin such an undertaking if it were about to disband.

At last he was given a few weeks of retreat before his profession in the order, which was set for January 16, 1842.

Once more, neither family nor old friends were with him to help celebrate his joy at his profession, which he made alone. He was the first priest received into the American branch of the order.

For a short time, he lived at Saint John's, Baltimore, which had been made the American motherhouse of the order. The priests who served the outlying areas lived there together and were able to observe their rule. John Neumann was happy even when he rode circuit to outlying missions. He had a home to come back to.

But trouble erupted in Pittsburgh. Fanned by the wind, fire, that ever-present menace, broke out in the city. Frame houses burst into flames. The few fire engines in the city could not cope with the blaze, and besides, they only fought the fires in the homes which were insured by the fire company. A poor man could not pay the fee of the fire company, and had to stand helplessly by while his house burned. Before the flames died down, a thousand homes were destroyed. How were the destitute going to pay their taxes? Saint Philomena's Church was in the process of being built by the Redemptorists for the German speaking parishioners who had flocked into the city. With no homes, often no jobs, and certainly no money, the parishioners could not support their church even if they were of a mind to. At this time of crisis, with the poor begging help and the church in debt, Father John Neumann was sent to the city to become pastor of Saint Philomena's

Church. Another man would have refused such an assignment, but not John Neumann. These people needed him. Paying little attention to finances, he first looked to the spiritual health of his flock. Beaten down with misfortune, they were near despair. He must give them hope and comfort. From his own experience, he knew that spiritual support of one another is essential, and he also knew that societies were dear to the heart of a German. He therefore inaugurated several pious societies where the members were united in prayer and also could enjoy some companionship. This idea grew and spread to other parishes. As for the debt, he organized groups to collect five cents or more a week from those who could pay. In this way, all had a share in building the church.

Never neglecting the children, he established three schools in the parish so that no child had to go too far to learn the ABC's and to study the catechism. Almost daily he could be found in one or another school, talking with the pupils, helping the teachers, or comforting an unhappy child.

Father Neumann had two assistants who were dedicated men. Together they managed to keep the Redemptorist rule of prayer. The pastor, however, saw that he carried the heaviest burden. If there were a sick call at night, he would rise and prepare to go.

"I need so little sleep," he would retort when the others protested. If he did not return until early in the morning, he would fill the coal scuttles, start the fires, then go into the church to pray until time for him to say the first Mass of the day.

Anti-Catholic feeling was very strong in the city. Fear of the immigrants and worry about the loss of jobs in time of crisis triggered some pockets of violence. Father Neumann experienced this when he answered a sick call one evening only to meet a man who beat him until he was badly bruised.

Then one of the schools was set on fire. "Thanks to the providence of God," Father Neumann wrote to his superior, "the blaze was discovered and put out before any great damage was done."

Although his first concern was his people, Father Neumann did manage to rescue the Church of Saint Philomena from its financial straits. Looking back on it he said, "I did nothing. Unless the faithful make use of it, the church is but a shell."

In his effort to help his people, the priest worked too hard, and as usual, ate too little. Exhausted, he became ill, but persisted in trying to do all the work. When his assistants saw that they did not have any influence on him, they wrote to their superior in Baltimore, telling him of the state of their pastor's health. The superior came to see him and was shocked at his frailness. "What good do you think you are doing by killing yourself?" he asked, looking sadly at the little man, for he was greatly worried about him. "We need your help for a long time. Your burdens must be shared. I am taking you back to Baltimore where I can make sure that you rest and recover."

So Father Neumann packed his bag and returned to the motherhouse in Baltimore.

CHAPTER EIGHT

UNSOUGHT RESPONSIBILITY

FATHER NEUMANN was grateful, in spite of himself, for the opportunity to rest, read and pray. For several years he had not been able to continue his study of Scripture, and he greatly regretted neglecting it. Quickly he fell into the routine of the house. Often he would wander into the kitchen to help the brother peel potatoes and prepare the dinner.

"It is such a relief to be nobody," he said one day. "No one asks my opinion of this or that, and I do not have to make money decisions."

"Watch out!" exclaimed the brother. "While you were so busy talking, you pared almost all that potato away."

John looked at the potato in dismay. "So I did! What a waste! I'll tell you brother, just put that little one on my plate tonight. I don't eat much anyway."

The brother grinned at him, "But I have the job of fattening you up. How can I do that if you won't eat?"

"If I get too fat, I won't fit into my clothes," retorted Father Neumann.

"That would be small loss," quipped the brother, "they are so worn out they are about to fall off you anyway."

For a few days, Father Neumann enjoyed the comradeship and pleasantries of his housemates. Then a letter for him arrived from Belgium, the headquarters for the American priests. It said that Father Neumann, only five years a Redemptorist, had been appointed vicegerent, or head of the American branch of the order.

"There must be some mistake. This can't be so," he exclaimed as he turned over the letter.

"It is true all right," said someone from the doorway. It was the present vicegerent, who too, had a letter in his hand. "This letter," and he waved it, "says I am to be relieved of my post and you are to succeed me."

Feeling that his predecessor had been happy in his post, Father Neumann looked at him sadly, feeling sorry for him and for himself. "I suppose we have no choice," he said.

"What a way to recuperate from an illness," thought Father Neumann. "It must be a grim joke." But he knew it was no joke. He had much to learn about the office before Father Czackert left for his new assignment.

The superiors in Belgium knew that the priests in the American foundation had been trying to do too many things at once. The vicegerent had pledged the order for more than it had men or money to handle. Since the superiors had learned how carefully Father Neumann had constructed Saint Philomena's Church in Pittsburgh, and knew of his great missionary work, they decided he was the right person to hold the office of vicegerent.

One of the great problems facing the Redemptorists was a German farming community near Erie, Pennsylvania. The settlement was named Saint Mary's, for the Blessed Virgin. In spite of the fact that a vast amount of money had been sent by the Leopoldine Society, the town did not prosper. It was far from the main means of transportation, and seemed to lack good leadership.

When he was appointed vicegerent, Father Neumann decided to put available funds elsewhere.

One summer day in 1847, a caller was announced at the rectory of Saint Alphonsus Church in Baltimore. It was Mother Theresa of the School Sisters of Notre Dame. Father Neumann, who had heard of the sisters' arrival in America, hurried to the parlor to greet the superior of the little group. In her black robes and starched white, Mother Theresa looked as crisp as though she had just stepped out of the cloister, instead of having traveled long distances.

"Mother Theresa, you are most welcome in America. We do need your help badly," he said, taking her hand.

"Father Neumann," she replied with a rueful smile, "You are the first to welcome us. All the others think us foolhardy to have come so far for no purpose."

Always ready to listen, the priest offered his visitor a chair, and settled down to give his full attention to the story. "Now, tell me your problems from the beginning."

"Baron von Schroeder was most persuasive. He came to see us many times, and assured us that all were anxiously awaiting us at Saint Mary's."

I know of the baron. He thinks if you settle at Saint Mary's, it will become a stable community."

"And, it is not?" questioned Mother Theresa.

"No, I am afraid it is not," replied Father Neumann. "The poverty is extreme. The town is not financially able to support you, and there are few children in the community. But whether or not you settle there is a decision you must make."

After a moment's thought, Mother Theresa said, "We will go there and find whether or not it is suitable for us. The money we have been given was earmarked for work at Saint Mary's. Our purpose is twofold. Besides educating children, we plan to open a motherhouse to train young ladies to add to our number."

A worried frown crossed Father Neumann's face. "Do keep in touch with me. I will help you all I can."

Mother Theresa rose. "You do not know how comforting you have been. I do not feel so abandoned. We will start for Saint Mary's as soon as practical."

Father Neumann gave his blessing for the journey. He knew the hardships that faced these women who had heretofore led such sheltered lives.

The first part of their journey took the group

by railway to the Susquehanna River, then on a steamboat up the river to the port where they could meet the stagecoach for Harrisburg.

On their arrival in Harrisburg, one of the sisters was taken violently ill and died before a priest or doctor could be summoned. Sadly, the sisters buried Sister Emmanuel in the new country and began the final stage of their 4,000 mile journey.

After traveling three days and two nights in an open wagon through almost impenetrable wilderness, they came to a clearing on which were perched a few shabby run-down houses. This was Saint Mary's. The Redemptorist fathers tried to make the sisters comfortable.

"We had no word from the bishop to expect you," said the pastor.

Mother Theresa looked at him in despair. "The baron told us that all formalities had been arranged."

"It is a long distance from Europe to America, and some tend to think that we dispense with all rules here. That is not true," explained Father Starck, who happened to be visiting Saint Mary's.

"Then, I must go see the bishop of Pittsburgh at once," said Mother Theresa.

The sisters began teaching the children immediately. Taking only a companion, Mother Theresa journeyed by wagon and rail to Pittsburgh. There she met Bishop O'Connor, who was most unhappy at the arrival of the nuns in his diocese.

"Mother Theresa, may I see your rule?" he asked abruptly.

The nun looked at him in dismay. "I do not

have it with me, Your Grace. I have always been accepted wherever I go, and am not in the habit of carrying it."

"You should," he growled. "Imposters are always showing up. I would like to see your rule."

"As soon as possible, I will send it to you. In the meantime, may we carry on our mission?"

"You may teach in Saint Mary's, but not in Pittsburgh until we can do away with the national parishes, and I do not know how soon that will be."

Having made his decision, he rose to dismiss the two sisters sitting before him.

The sisters decided that they needed the advice of their only friend, Father Neumann. They took the train to Baltimore, where on arrival they went directly to Saint Alphonsus rectory.

Father Neumann listened sympathetically to the account of their troubles. He promised to say a Mass for Sister Emmanuel, then said, "There is a building in my own parish, Saint James, that I think would fit your needs. Would you like to see it?"

Mother Theresa rose quickly. "Can we go immediately?"

"As soon as I get my hat." Father Neumann had a twinkle in his eye. At last he was about to see one of his dreams come true. He had prayed for sisters to staff his schools and here, from Munich, were the School Sisters of Notre Dame ready and willing to begin immediately.

As they walked down the road to the building that until recently had housed the Redemptorist

Novitiate, Father Neumann unfolded his plan of having the sisters teach in the Baltimore schools of Saint James and Saint Alphonsus.

Mother Theresa found the building most suitable, bought it from the Redemptorists and sent for the sisters in Saint Mary's to return to Baltimore, where the community grew under Father Neumann's guidance.

Shortly after Father Neumann's appointment, the superior of their branch of the Redemptorists came from Belgium to visit the American houses. He was shocked at the amount of money several priests had made themselves responsible for. A strict observer of the rule, he was afraid that the air of freedom and spirit of progress in America would hamper prayer. He knew that the crushing debts could not help but preoccupy the minds of the priests. He was aware that the members of his order were only trying as best they could to be of help. American bishops were so short of German speaking priests that they urged those they met to stay and build churches. It was hard not to respond to their pleas.

The only way that the superior saw to preserve the Redemptorist rule was to lay down some strict regulations. He limited the money the priests could contract to spend without special permission. He also restricted journeys. (Father Neumann could have wished that this rule had been in force earlier.) The priests under Father Neumann found it hard to obey these instructions.

The bishop of New Orleans built a church and invited a Redemptorist to come. The superior said he was needed elsewhere and Father Neumann backed him up.

A priest in New York wanted to build another church and did so over Father Neumann's objections. He found the priests as hard to handle as the trustees in Rochester.

"I do not like telling older and wiser priests what to do," he said to his friend Father Pax who was visiting him.

Those men who had come to America originally and those who came later had much more experience than their new superior.

Father Pax encouraged him. "Someone has to do it. And since you have been lawfully appointed without seeking the office, I can see no reason for you to excuse yourself from the burden."

"You are right," agreed his friend, "but it is not my choice — in fact, I was never asked to make a choice, so I will do the best I can."

Father Neumann carefully carried out the orders given him. Those who did not like his ruling often wrote to Belgium, and some wrote to the main monastery in Austria and complained.

In the meantime, as often as he could, Father Neumann visited the schools and parishes, and at home acted as though he were one of the humblest of lay brothers.

One morning he appeared at the door of the Redemptorist house in New York and asked to see the pastor. As the new porter went to call him, Father Neumann started to follow.

Turning to him the young man said, "Stay here, if you please. Take a seat on that bench, while I call the superior." As he left, he muttered, "This man thinks he can enter the cloister."

In a few minutes, he was back. "What is your name?"

"I am Father Neumann," was the reply.

"Oh, if you are one of the priests, do come in," the porter said, and led him to the superior's office. His mouth fell in astonishment when he saw the superior come forward and kneel to ask Father Neumann's blessing. The poor porter beat a hasty retreat.

Later Father Neumann sent for the young man and told him that he had faithfully performed his job of porter, but added with a smile, "I think it might be wise not to think out loud."

Having applied for American citizenship some years previously, the priest was now eligible to be sworn in. Down at the court house, in company with a great crowd of immigrants, John Neumann held up his right hand and swore to be a dutiful son of America. This vow he fulfilled in every way he could. The children, as always, were in his thoughts. "They are the hope of our nation," he repeated often.

In Baltimore there was a settlement of refugees who had fled Santo Domingo during the uprising in the 1820's. A Father Joubert tried to teach the children their catechism, but found it difficult because they could neither read nor write. To help him in this work, he recruited a congregation of black women who took the title of the Oblate Sisters of Providence. These sisters taught the children and conducted an orphanage. After

Father Joubert's death, no one offered the sisters spiritual guidance, nor advised them in their problems. Father Neumann learned that the sisters were in trouble and visited them.

"I will come regularly to give you help," he promised.

When he became vicegerent of the Redemptorists, he sent one of his best men, Father Anwander, to be their counselor. The bishop, having heard of the plight of the sisters, wanted to disband the order, but Father Anwander went to him and pleaded that they be given another chance. The bishop listened and allowed the sisters to continue their work. Today, thanks to Father Neumann, the Oblate Sisters of Providence are working in many dioceses throughout the United States.

Revolution once again hit Europe. The Austrian houses of the Redemptorists were confiscated. Father Passerat, the vicar-general, and the priests fled to Belgium. On his arrival at the monastery, Father Passerat wrote to Father Neumann that he was designating America a province, and appointed Father Neumann its superior.

At that time, there was a new superior of the Belgium Redemptorists, who was not as sympathetic to the American's problems as his predecessor. As soon as he heard what Father Passerat had done, he went to him and said:

"This appointment is illegal. You did not have the consent of your two consultors. They have not reached our monastery as yet."

"I know," replied Father Passerat, "but there

are times when it is necessary to act quickly, without consulting the rules. No one knows where my two consultors are. As you well know, many priests have been imprisoned or killed, and they may be among them. You read Father Neumann's letter."

Father Neumann had written, "As vicegerent, I am forced to write for permission for only slight things that could be settled in America. Under these circumstances, I cannot rule with authority. Often, long before I can get a reply, the damage has been done."

Father Heilig, the Belgian superior, did not think that reason enough to break the rules. The dispute was referred to the head of the order in Rome. The authorities decided that America should be made a province, but placed the appointment in the hands of the superior in Belgium.

By that time, some disgruntled priests whom Father Neumann had been forced to restrain had written long and often to Father Heilig, the superior in Belgium, complaining about their vicegerent.

Father Heilig, influenced by their complaints, and thinking the dissatisfaction was wide-spread, wrote to Father Neumann, saying "I cannot conceal from you, and I believe Your Reverence freely admits, that you have to contend with strong opposition from our men in America. . . . For your sake, and in the best interests of the whole congregation in America, it might be well to consider whether it would be better to decline the appointment as vice-provincial of your own accord."

Actually a few days earlier, Father Neumann had written a letter begging to be relieved of his office. As soon as he heard from Father Heilig, he wrote again expressing his great desire to step down. In the meantime, Father Fey had reached Belgium from America and explained the true state of the order and that only a few men who were restrained were loud in their complaints. Father Heilig appointed a priest from Belgium as vice-provincial, but wrote to Father Neumann a note of apology that he had acted hastily. He said, "I made a mistake if I overrated the opposition which I believed existed against you."

Not caring in the least why he had been relieved of his office, John Neumann was delighted to once again be a "nobody." When he left office, there were ten religious houses and the number of priests had grown to thirty. There was no doubt that during his term of office, the missions had been solidified both spiritually and financially.

That some might think he had been demoted did not worry Father Neumann one bit.

"If I had been the superior-general, I never would have appointed any one with so little to recommend him," he told his brother Wenzel. Then he added with the usual twinkle in his eyes, "I guess you can put that down to human error in judgment."

Father Neumann's days were never meant to be spent in meditation. When the new superior arrived, he immediately appointed his predecessor to be one of his two consultors, and also to be pastor of the new St. Alphonsus Church in Baltimore.

During his first assignment to the Buffalo area,
the missionary had written a catechism in German
for the children in his class. For the children
of Baltimore, he rewrote and published this
catechism, which became the standard text for
teaching religion in all German Catholic schools.

Using his talent for writing, he contributed a
number of articles on theology to German
magazines.

His superior discussed with him the formation
of a group of preachers. Father Neumann was
delighted. "Now that we have more experienced
men coming from Europe, and a group of edu-
cated, enthusiastic American priests, I think we
could begin sending out bands of preachers to
parishes to increase the fervor of the people. Will
you help to organize them?" asked the superior.

Father Neumann did this gladly. Sometimes he
accompanied a group, not to preach, but to hear
confessions and to counsel.

An American Redemptorist seminary was also
one of his aims. During this period of comparative
leisure, he talked about it, and begged for it until
he saw the first American house of studies for
Redemptorists established in Cumberland, Maryland.

With Wenzel's arrival in America, John Neumann felt that surely they would get word from
his family. This was not the case. Not in all his
years in America had one of their letters reached
him. Both he and his brother wrote regularly,
and they knew that somewhere a pile of letters
was awaiting them.

In a letter written in 1851, he expressed as usual his devotion to his family. "My beloved Father and dear sisters," he wrote. "Brother Wenzel and I had given up all hope of ever hearing from our dear home, when we were most unexpectedly rejoiced by the arrival of a letter from our dear cousin, George Zahn, and another, a short time ago, from Sister Caroline. We have long anxiously desired to hear from home. I cannot conceive how your letters could have gone astray. It would be a great consolation to us to know the date of our dear mother's death, also that of our sister Veronica. . . ."

These were rewarding days for Father Neumann. He always found time to visit the schools and help the School Sisters of Notre Dame, whom he had taken under his special care.

He also spent long hours in the confessional. Many came to him regularly. Among those who had made him their confessor was the newly appointed archbishop of Baltimore and dean of the American bishops, Archbishop Francis P. Kenrick, recently come from his post as bishop of Philadelphia.

Archbishop Kenrick became fast friends with his confessor. He recognized Father Neumann as a holy man who was quite capable of managing affairs.

One of the problems weighing on the archbishop's mind was that of a successor in Philadelphia. He frequently discussed this with his confessor. "The debts I left behind in Philadelphia haunt me. I do wish I had not been forced to leave the diocese in such financial straits."

"Why are there such large debts, Your Grace?"

"One reason is the cathedral. Philadelphians think big, but they are not so quick to dig into their pockets. There it stands, only the walls erected. There is no roof, no facade and no money to pay for them. Father Edmund Waldron, who is in charge, is quite put out with me."

"Why?"

"He did not think I pushed it hard enough. But there are other worthy causes, for instance, the seminary to train the priests the city needs so badly."

"And do you know," the archbishop leaned forward and tapped Father Neumann on the knee, "those Germans" — at Father Neumann's slight frown, he continued with a smile — "those Germans in my parish got together and wrote to the Leopoldine Society."

"Yes?"

"They want all the money sent for the missions to be spent on the Germans. I guess we Irish have no souls to be saved." At that quip, the archbishop sat back and grinned broadly.

"Oh no, Your Grace," Father Neumann protested. "Sometimes, money collected for a special purpose has not been spent wisely. It is a sacred trust when one solicits funds for a certain reason that it be spent in the spirit that it has been given. The German people donated to the Leopoldine Foundation for the express purpose of helping their relatives and friends who have come to America."

"I can see their point even though it limits charity," agreed the bishop. Then he added, "We should have a German bishop and then they would be satisfied."

"Poor soul," John commiserated with the hypothetical bishop. "He would have a difficult time keeping control."

Looking closely at Father Neumann, the archbishop said, "I think you are the right German for the bishopric of Philadelphia."

Horrified, Father Neumann sprang to his feet. "Please Your Grace, don't even say so in jest."

"I am not jesting, Father. I am warning you that your name is among the three I have sent to Rome."

"Oh, I beg you, recall it, I cannot accept. I am not capable." Wringing his hands, he paced the room.

"You can and must accept if you are appointed. It will be your duty. Think it over, Father." The archbishop picked up his hat, and bade Father Neumann good-bye.

So distraught was he that he scarcely heard the archbishop leave.

Immediately, he sat down to write to the Redemptorist superior in Rome. "Go, ask to see the pope. Explain to him that I am a poor unprepossessing little priest, totally unable to fill such a high office."

Bishop of Philadelphia! That was one of the most important sees in all America. That would be as absurd as to appoint him bishop of Prague, or of Paris. It just could not be! He put on his hat and went to see the School Sisters of Notre Dame and the Oblates of Divine Providence and begged each that they and their children start to pray immediately to ward off a great disaster that threatened to befall the Church in America.

Calmed by the thought of their prayers, he walked home. Even if Archbishop Kenrick thought him capable, he reasoned, there were others of better judgment in this case, who surely would not agree. He could count on their voting against him.

In Rome, the pope held several consultations. In spite of some dissenting opinions, he finally decided to appoint John Neumann to the see of Philadelphia.

When Archbishop Kenrick received the news, he went to see his confessor. Receiving no answer to his knock, the archbishop entered the room and left on the priest's desk the pectoral cross and the ring he had worn when bishop of Philadelphia.

Seeing something glitter that evening as he lit the candle to study, Father Neumann picked up the cross. Immediately he knew what it meant. Unwilling to believe it, he looked for the lay brother who had been in the house all day.

"Who was in my room today?" he asked.

"No one, Father, except the archbishop. He only stopped for a minute. I thought he wanted to leave something."

"He did," moaned Father Neumann. "He left me a greater burden than I can bear."

Thanking the brother, he went to his room where he prayed all night for comfort and guidance.

CHAPTER NINE

A PRINCE OF THE CHURCH

"I COMMAND Father Neumann under formal obedience to accept the diocese of Philadelphia without further appeal," were the words used by Pope Pius IX in making his appointment.

Although stricken at the news, Father Neumann had no choice. He feared that he could not perform the office correctly, and also thought that it would increase his difficulty in finding time for his own sanctification. "I would rather die tomorrow than be consecrated bishop," he told one of his friends. However, he bowed to the will of the pope and accepted the honor with his usual good grace.

There was much talk and wagging of heads at the news. King Louis of Bavaria was delighted that one so devoted to education should receive the appointment. Philip Neumann, now an old man, could not be convinced that his little quiet Johnny was to become a great bishop. He accused those that came to tell him of making fun of him. Reluctantly he believed, when he had a letter from his own son. Even then, he went about, shaking his head.

"My little boy, my humble son, a great bishop of the church! Only a few years ago, he told me with tears in his eyes that he did not want to be a stocking knitter. Just imagine! My boy a bishop!"

Indeed, the turn of events was incredible. The Germans thought that they would get preferential treatment, but they did not know their man. For years, John Neumann had studied languages so that he could help all people. Long ago, he had learned a few words of the Mohawk Indian dialect. Since then he had added Spanish and Gaelic to his store of knowledge. He belonged to all people. No one had preference.

The day selected for the consecration of Bishop Neumann was March 28, 1852, only nine days after word of his appointment had been received. Because the First Plenary Council of Baltimore was about to be convened, and Archbishop Kenrick wanted his friend John to participate, no time was lost in installing the new bishop.

Although preparations were hurried, the ceremony was carried out with fitting dignity. A huge procession of 1,500 members of societies, school children and dignitaries wended its way from the episcopal residence to Saint Alphonsus Church, where, until that day, Father Neumann had been pastor. Accompanying the new bishop of Philadelphia were Archbishop Kenrick, his old friend; Father Bernard O'Reilly from Rochester, now bishop of Hartford, Connecticut; and Father L'Homme, president of Saint Mary's Seminary, Baltimore and vicar-general of that city.

In all the crowded church there was no one to represent his family. Wenzel, now a lay brother working in Detroit, had been given permission to attend the ceremonies, but because of the expense to the order, thought it best not to come. Once again, John felt keenly not having the support of his family.

When during the ceremonies, the pectoral cross was put around his neck and the bishop's ring placed on his finger Bishop Neumann felt great sadness and a sense of assuming an intolerable burden. How could he carry on the work to which he had been called?

Having preached a farewell to his congregation that night and accepted their good wishes, he spent the next day visiting his schools and his fellow Redemptorists. When they admired his episcopal robes, he said, "The church treats her bishops like a mother treats a child. When she wants to put a burden on him, she gives him new clothes."

Before the consecration, Archbishop Kenrick and he had talked often about the diocese of Philadelphia and the problems to be solved.

"Philadelphia is only part of your problem. Your flock is widely scattered through the countryside. Many days you will spend jouncing along behind a plodding horse," said the archbishop.

"That I am used to, and the railroads will make my trips easier. Imagine traveling at twenty-five miles an hour! Think of the time it will save me."

"Yes," said the archbishop with a twinkle in

his eye, "you will have more time for receptions and meetings with creditors."

Even though he was aware that the good Irish archbishop could not lose an opportunity to tease, Bishop Neumann shuddered because he knew the remark was only too true.

A delegation from Philadelphia had come to Baltimore for the consecration. Father Edward Sourin, administrator of the diocese of Philadelphia, had preached at the ceremony. This priest, whom Bishop Neumann later named his vicar-general, offered his ready support. He knew that the bishop was aware of the subtle opposition to his appointment and that he shrank from display. Father Sourin suggested that the new bishop be welcomed by a school built in his honor rather than by a large reception.

To Bishop Neumann's surprise, when he and his escorts stepped from the train in Philadelphia, they were met by a large delegation of clergy and laymen who escorted him to his new home on Logan Square.

As soon as the dignitaries had left, Bishop Neumann hurried to an upstairs window where he could peer at the roofless cathedral, which was to be the source of great anxiety to him.

As he turned from the window with a sigh, Father Waldron, who was in charge of building the cathedral, came up behind him. "Tomorrow, your Grace, I will take you all over the cathedral and show you the plans. It is our first priority. Within a year it can be completed. All we need is your signature to borrow the funds to finish it. May I come for you tomorrow at eleven?"

"Not tomorrow, I am afraid. There are too many commitments. I can see a good deal of your problems from here. We will talk about the cathedral later," he said kindly.

But Father Waldron, whose whole heart and time were wrapped up in the new church, felt rebuffed. He knew the cathedral would not be the bishop's first worry.

Within two weeks, the new bishop had written a pastoral letter to be read in all the parishes. In it he mentioned the need for a fitting house of God such as the cathedral, the value of schools and his hope for increased fervor in all. Then he explained the purpose of the First National Council of Bishops and asked for prayers for its success.

The Fourth Sunday after Easter found the new bishop returning to Baltimore to attend the Council.

"I was so anxious for your consecration," the archbishop told him, "because I wanted you to participate in this council."

The city of Baltimore did all it could to honor such an important body of church leaders. Each was met at the train by a special committee and escorted to the hotel where he was treated to every courtesy. Left to himself, Bishop Neumann would have quietly come into the city and without escort have carried his bag himself as he walked to the Redemptorist house. But now he was the distinguished representative from Philadelphia.

Thirty-one American bishops attended the council. Of these, two-thirds were foreign-born—Irish, French, Spanish, and one Bohemian, who looking around found himself the least of them. There was no doubt that he had been the last to be appointed to such a position. Since he was so new, Bishop Neumann did more listening than talking.

On his return to Philadelphia, the bishop immediately took up the problems of schools. He wrote all the pastors requesting them to meet with him and to bring two representative laymen from each parish. At this meeting, he set up a school board to establish standards so that education would become as good in one parish as another. Thus he is credited with establishing a parochial school system.

Bishop Neumann was adamant on some subjects, the first being the education of children. Most pastors gladly swung into line, as they sought help in the best methods of teaching their children. A few did not agree, and did nothing.

One pastor kept putting off beginning a school and replied to inquiries from the bishop by saying: "It is impossible just now."

Having heard this excuse several times, the bishop replied firmly, "If it is impossible for you to establish a school, I shall look for another to fill your place. He will perhaps find it possible to secure a Christian education for the children of this parish."

Heeding this word of warning, the pastor opened a school, which enrolled one thousand pupils the first day.

As always, the people were the first concern of the new bishop. He met them wherever he could. Philadelphia was social, and the leading prelate of the diocese was often invited to social functions. Bishop Neumann avoided as many as he could, but when forced to attend, he was gracious. Prominent Catholics did not think their new bishop, a shabby little man, would represent them well, but when they saw him in animated conversation, first with the French ambassador, then with an Italian delegate, both in their own language, they began to revise their opinions.

Still devoted to the Redemptorist rule, Bishop Neumann walked each week to Saint Peter's Church to make his confession, and often would stay for supper. When first consecrated, the bishop retained his Redemptorist habit, but, finding that some objected, he began to wear his episcopal robes. In the rectory at Saint Peter's, however, he once more donned the habit.

Often, after joining with his brothers in singing vespers and dining with them, he would disappear. The rector always knew where to find him. Back in the kitchen, an apron around his waist, he would be exchanging jokes with a lay brother while drying dishes.

Unfortunately, all his relations with the Germans were not so relaxed. Once more he ran into the problem of trusteeism. The situation at Trinity Church had become so bad that Archbishop Kenrick, when he was bishop of Philadelphia, had been forced to close the church. Outraged, the trustees took the diocese to court. The case was pending when the new bishop arrived. Bishop Neumann, who had been so successful with other trustees, could not move this group. Not expecting to have a quick settlement of the case, and concerned about the German speaking people who had settled in South and Central Philadelphia, he began building Saint Alphonsus Church. Labor costs were high and the church became a financial burden. Father Waldron saw funds needed for the cathedral being diverted to Saint Alphonsus, and protested.

"But," the bishop told him, "these funds were never earmarked for the cathedral except in your imagination. Money is desperately needed for a church for these people. You may take up collections and ask for donations for the cathedral, but until you have the money in hand, I want no more building."

Since priests were so scarce, Bishop Neumann knew that one of the first things he must do was to see that the seminary Bishop Kenrick had begun was properly cared for. The Vincentian fathers who had staffed the college were called by their superiors to serve elsewhere. The bishop had to find good men to supplant them. He named Father William O'Hara rector, and supplied teachers of superior knowledge. Often Bishop Neumann himself gave retreats to the students and to the priests.

When at home, he spent long hours in the confessional. Many days, however, he went out of town to visit parishes scattered throughout his 35,000 square-mile diocese, which included besides the eastern half of Pennsylvania, the entire state of Delaware and the southern half of New

Jersey. At each church, he carefully examined church records and finances, offered advice to pastors, listened to parishioners, heard as many confessions as he could, preached and administered the sacrament of Confirmation.

As he traveled from place to place, he became convinced that the diocese was too large for one man to handle. Since he had no assistants, work in Philadelphia had to come to a standstill while he was away, yet it was necessary for him to make these arduous trips. To relatives in Bohemia he wrote, "A bishop in America has to do everything himself and by his own hand. I have been interrupted twenty times in writing this two-page letter."

Always a devotee of the Blessed Sacrament, Bishop Neumann loved a devotion begun in Europe some years back. It was called "The Forty Hours" devotion in honor of the forty hours Christ spent in the tomb. For that length of time, the Blessed Sacrament was solemnly exposed on the altar of a church, while private and public devotions were performed.

At a meeting of the priests in his diocese, he introduced the idea of a diocesanwide celebration of the Forty Hours, each church taking a turn so that it would be celebrated somewhere in the area every week. Since anti-Catholic feeling ran high at that time, many prudent priests thought that there was real danger that the Blessed Sacrament would be desecrated. Bishop Neumann thought differently. One night, he sat down to write a letter to each parish to say that he would like

each to consider taking a turn at the celebration.
Having worked long hours, he fell asleep in his
chair. When he woke, he saw to his dismay that
the candle he was using for heating his sealing
wax had toppled on top of his letters. Instead of
setting all the papers ablaze, it had charred the
paper around the words that the Forty Hours
were to be observed in every parish. Falling to
his knees in astonishment, he seemed to hear a
voice that said: "As the flames are burning here
without consuming or injuring the writing, so
shall I pour out my Grace in the Blessed Sacrament without prejudice to my honor. Fear no
profanation, therefore; hesitate no longer to carry
out your design for My Glory."

Taking this as a sign, Bishop Neumann set up
the schedule for Forty Hours. It has been observed
since that time in every parish in the diocese, and
the practice has spread throughout the United
States. As he continued on his diocesan visits, he
preached on the value of this devotion.

On his return from one of his trips to outlying
parishes, he found awaiting him a special invitation from Pope Pius IX to be present in Rome
when the Immaculate Conception of the Mother
of God was declared an article of faith. Could he
afford to go? As usual, in his personal poverty
he had no money to spend. But, he had to go to
Rome for his visit to the pope. And this trip
meant that he could go to see his father also.
What an unexpected blessing!

CHAPTER TEN

A JOYFUL PILGRIMAGE

AS OFTEN as he could, Bishop Neumann slipped away from his home on Logan Square to join his fellow Redemptorists. After dinner one evening, as he and his confreres settled in their chairs in the recreation room of Saint Peter's rectory, the bishop announced to them, "I'm going to Rome! Just think of it! Going to Rome! When I came over here, I had no hope of returning to Europe, much less of traveling to Rome to take part in the ceremony of proclaiming the dogma of the Immaculate Conception of Mary."

Knowing full well that he would never mention it, the rector broke in with, "The pope sent a special invitation to the bishop by Archbishop Kenrick."

Brushing off the exclamations of congratulations, Bishop Neumann said, "He knew I would have to come sooner or later on the visit required of every bishop. Now I can combine both and save the diocese some money."

"You deserve a little change," said one of the fathers. "You work day and night. Don't worry about the cost."

"If those who are pressing for a roof on the cathedral heard you say that, they would disagree," replied the bishop.

"I know," persisted the priest, "but your trip would not put too many tiles on the roof."

"Then," added the bishop, "there are some who think the proclamation is unnecessary. In one of the Irish parishes an old man came up to me and said, 'Now Fayther why are we having all this foolishness about something we've always believed!' "

The Irish brogue with which he told the story made everyone laugh, but they agreed that the old man had a point. This was not a new article of faith.

Careful plans were made for the trip. While in Europe, Bishop Neumann hoped to visit his eighty-year-old father and his sisters. He would miss seeing his mother, who had died several years earlier. Both John Neumann and the townfolk of Prachatitz were looking forward to this visit. Prachatitz had never before been able to claim such a distinguished person as a native son. In his quiet way, the bishop thought he could slip in and out of town unnoticed.

There were other reasons for making this trip. He needed to recruit priests and seminarians for his diocese. He also intended to beg for money. America was still a mission country. The majority of parishioners were poor. Those who came from a country where Catholicism was a state religion were used to the government supporting the church and did not contribute much.

As Bishop Neumann stood at the rail of the *S. S. Union* and watched the shores of America fade, he thought of his first glimpse of New York from the rail of the immigrant ship. What had the Lord done to him? A young man with only one dollar in his pocket, his clothes ragged, was returning dressed as a bishop, traveling in comfort in a cabin of his own. He looked to heaven and prayed that his head would not be turned with all this pomp. After all, deep down he was only a poor Bohemian man, trying to do the will of God as he saw it.

Although it took only seventeen days, the crossing was bad, and few passengers joined him as he walked the decks. All were grateful when the ship entered the harbor at Le Havre. What fantastic advances had been made in the past two decades! Instead of walking and riding stagecoaches to reach the port, he now went across France by train. True, the ride was dirty, and most of the time the travelers were covered by cinders and their hands and faces smudged by soot, but the little engines puffed along and finally they reached Marseilles.

At that French port, Bishop Neumann took ship with several other bishops traveling to Rome. When they arrived at Civitá Vecchia, Bishop Neumann's mind turned to Saint Paul arriving in chains at Pozzuoli, enroute to Rome. "If it had not been for Saint Paul and Saint Peter who had arrived in Rome before me," Bishop Neumann thought, "I might not be here today." But, then he said to himself, "God would have had His

will even if He had to use different men. I am
not important. What is important is the work I
have been given to do."

When they disembarked, the bishops each went
his own way knowing they would meet at the
great ceremonies at the Vatican on December 8th.

Waiting at the dock to greet Bishop Neumann
were several of his fellow Redemptorists who had
worked with him in America. They took him to
their monastery where he lived for two months.

Quickly he settled into the routine of the order.
Daily he roamed on foot through the winding
streets of Rome. The four great Churches of
Rome, Saint Mary Major, Saint Paul's Outside
the Walls, Saint John Lateran and Saint Peter's,
he visited often and said Mass there. Dressed in
the plain habit worn by Redemptorist priests, he
made no effort to let others know he was a
bishop. On clear days, he often had a companion
on his walks, but on those days that rain slashed
through the canyons made by the tightly packed
houses, he was left alone to make his way through
the mud and puddles.

At last, the time for the four-day consistory
arrived. Then the bishop of Philadelphia was
arrayed as befitting his office. He endured the gold
encrusted vestments with the same good will
with which he had accepted the rain and mud.
He looked around at the fifty-three cardinals and
his fellow bishops and rejoiced that he could join
in this beautiful occasion. He wrote to a friend,
"I thank God He allowed me to see this day in
Rome."

Shortly after the celebration, Pope Pius IX had time for an audience with Bishop Neumann. Together they discussed the problems of the diocese and the progress made. Bishop Neumann was able to report that fifty new churches had been opened, and a school system established which in a three-year period had grown in enrollments from six hundred to nine thousand students. Sadly he told the pope that there was no roof on the cathedral and that the diocese was still in debt, mostly due to the trouble he had had with the trustees in Trinity Church. "What bothers me especially," he said with a slight grimace, "is that Your Holiness thought a German speaking bishop was needed to help the Germans, and it is one of their parishes which has given me so many heartaches.

"There is also great need for an orphanage for German children," Bishop Neumann continued. "I had hoped that some Dominican sisters might be persuaded to come to America to help."

The pope nodded sympathetically.

"And, finally, Your Holiness," continued the bishop, "a letter from one of my priests has just arrived. He says that there are three ladies under his guidance who would like to join together in a religious society to help the poor."

The pope smiled. "You have here the solution to your problem. Why not interest these young women in becoming sisters of the Third Order of Saint Francis? They could staff your new orphanage. You have my permission to establish the order."

Delighted with this idea Bishop Neumann resolved that one of his first calls on his return would be on these young women.

The pope was pleased with the report of the Philadelphia diocese and told the bishop that he had confidence in him.

"Your Holiness," he replied, "I will do all in my power to fulfill the office."

With the pope's blessing ringing in his ears, Bishop Neumann left the Vatican, packed his bag at the Redemptorist house, and started on his journey home.

Railroads had not yet penetrated to all parts of Europe, so Bishop Neumann rode the stage to Loreto. There he visited the Basilica that held the house of the Holy Family which had been miraculously transported from Nazareth to Dalmatia and then to Loreto.

On the road to Bologna, his carriage was stopped by the border guard. The only pair of shoes the bishop owned had been worn out by his tramps through the streets of Rome. His coat and cloak were shabby. The officer, not being able to read the papers written in English, roughly ordered him to the guard house for questioning. Since the snow was deep and he would have been very wet by the time he floundered through it, he quietly produced his bishop's cross and ring. The first reaction was disbelief, but when the guard saw the proof, he apologized in great confusion and begged the "Right Reverend Sir" not to report him to the authorities.

Smiling at him, the bishop said, "Many people make the same mistake about me. I know I do not look like a bishop. Most are taller and fatter. I am too small and thin to be a good bishop."

Once he had put the guard at his ease, he continued his journey, and shortly thereafter he greeted his old friend Adalbert Schmidt, who was now the director of the seminary at Gratz.

When Adalbert started to kneel to kiss the bishop's ring, John Neumann stopped him in great distress. "Please, old friend," he begged, "do not embarrass me so." And he put his arms around Adalbert in a big hug.

"John, John, you will never change," replied Adalbert returning the hug. "How I have missed you. I should have gone to America with you, but then," he added, "we would not be here now. We couldn't both be bishop."

"You would have been, Adalbert. How I wish you had come to America. By now you would be bishop and I would not have to carry the burden of the mitre."

"You have not changed one bit," said Adalbert with affection. "At heart you were always a simple priest."

"And I pray I continue so until the day I die," answered the bishop. But brightening, he said, "Come, give me the news of your family, and all you have been doing since I left here. From what I can gather you have not been without honors."

The few days the old friends had together went all too quickly. They laughed over John's horsemanship, and Adalbert exclaimed over the descriptions of that vast country his friend now claimed as home.

At last it was time to leave. His next stop would be Prague. There Father Dichtl would meet him, and he would see his sister Joan, now Mother Caroline of the Sisters of Saint Charles Borromeo.

As the coach took Bishop Neumann over the Charles IV bridge into Prague, he resolved to find time to walk over the ancient structure as he had done so often as a student. He wanted to stand on the spot where his patron Saint John Nepomucene had been martyred. Many times as a student, before he could even dream of being a bishop, he had stood on this spot and looked down at the river. On arriving in the city, he went first to the Convent of the Sisters of Saint Charles. His sister Joan greeted him with great joy. She told him all the news about the family. "And Wenzel, how is he?" she asked thinking of the baby brother they had all loved so dearly.

"He is well, and doing more than his share to help where the laborers are few."

"My sisters and I will come, too," offered Mother Caroline.

The bishop smiled. "You anticipated my request. I need you in Philadelphia. It is a civilized city. You would not experience the hazards of the wilderness."

Reluctantly he bid his sister good-bye, gave her his blessing and set out to meet Father Dichtl. He felt close to this priest, who alone, years ago saw that he had to go to America, had supported his pleas, and had encouraged him at every step.

Together they walked to the various shrines of familiar saints. They stopped in front of the famous astronomical clock which had been set in motion in the 15th century and had been keeping time in front of the town hall ever since. The hour was about to strike so they awaited the appearance of the large figures of our Lord and the apostles.

As they were waiting with townsfolk to see the sight, Bishop Neumann remarked, "How different this is from America. There this clock would long since have been torn down and replaced with something new."

"Life there is very different, I can see," remarked his friend, "but deep down people are the same."

As they were returning to the rectory, Father Dichtl clapped his hand to his head. "How could I have forgotten? In the excitement of seeing you it slipped my mind, but I have been bidden to bring you tonight to dine with the ex-Emperor Ferdinand in his palace."

John Neumann looked at his friend with dismay. "We were to have an evening together, you and I. Can we possibly not go?"

"Not in this country." Father Dichtl looked at his friend and noted his distress. "You have lived too long in America, where all men are equal."

"I suppose so," said the bishop in a tone of resignation. "I know that when emperors, or ex-emperors invite, even princes of the church accept. I will go."

Actually, the emperor was gracious and all the company was interested in the happenings in that vast country across the water. They all exclaimed at the hazards of sailing the ocean. The ladies asked questions about dress and customs that the bishop found a bit difficult to answer. The meal was sumptuous. Course followed course. As usual. Bishop Neumann ate little. Time came for the dessert.

"I hear that you scarcely ever eat sweets, your Lordship," said Ferdinand, "but I have had a special Bohemian treat prepared for you which I hope you will find agreeable to your taste."

He gave a signal to the head waiter who put directly before the bishop a huge covered silver dish.

Realizing its contents would be enough to serve ten people, Bishop Neumann looked inquiringly at the emperor, who nodded again. With a flourish, the waiter lifted the lid to display a bowl filled to overflowing with American gold coins.

"What generosity!" murmured the bishop as he touched a coin. These will provide food, both spiritual and temporal, for the poor in my flock and even put a tile or two on the roof of the cathedral."

The next day as he trudged across the Charles IV bridge to the spot, marked with a marble slab, between the sixth and seventh pillars, where Saint John Nepomucene had been pushed to his death, John thanked God for Prague and all its inhabitants, from Emperor Ferdinand to the lowliest citizen.

Even though he was anxious to reach home, it

was necessary to save some time to visit his old seminary. Some of his friends were now teaching there. As a token of their esteem he was presented with a chalice that seemed to be intertwined with the Irish and Bohemian as was now the bishop's life in his diocese. On the inside rim of the chalice, made in Prague, was the inscription "In 1686 friends have wrought me through the agency of Father Peter O'Kearney."

With his bags weighed down with the precious chalice, the money donated by the emperor and supplemented by others, and the relics and medals he had collected on the way, Bishop Neumann set out for Prachatitz. Shortly he would be home, but first he must stop to see the new bishop of Budweis.

Having visited for a few days in the city where he had studied, he announced one evening that he would go to Prachatitz the next day.

"I will send you in my sleigh," said Bishop Iirisik.

John had seen the sleigh and the handsome pair of horses. At the sight of his son in such an equipage his father would surely have a stroke.

"Thank you, Sir," he said, "but such a magnificent sleigh and those beautiful horses are too fine for a missionary bishop such as I. My people in Prachatitz will think I have become too proud for them. I prefer to go there unnoticed."

"As you wish, your Grace, but you are most welcome to use them."

"A simple entry into the town would be better, I am sure," the bishop insisted.

The next day a modest closed sleigh drew up

to the door of the residence of the bishop of Budweis. Bishop Neumann and his nephew John Berger, who had come to the city to meet him, climbed in and pulled up the robe. At this, a young man who had been loitering across the road started off at a good pace for Prachatitz. The townsfolk knew their man well and did not intend to permit him to come home unannounced.

All along the route, the boy alerted the villagers. As the sleigh came abreast of each hamlet, all the inhabitants were out to greet him. He was forced to stop to speak to the people and to give his blessing. When they reached the town of Nettolitz, halfway home, he was persuaded to spend the night.

To John Berger, he said, "Tomorrow we will send the sleigh ahead and cut across the mountains. I know every step of the way, I've walked it often enough. It will take only three hours, and we will enter the city from the opposite direction than by which they will expect us."

Their plans were futile. The villagers kept close watch. After Mass the next morning, cut off from escape, they were led to the magnificent sleigh of the Prince of Schwarzenberg with four spirited horses and liveried attendants. Although greatly disturbed by such display, the bishop was forced to use the sleigh. Outside their home town they were met by a procession of dignitaries of both church and state and led into the city square.

When they passed under the gate, the bishop looked over his shoulder to see the picture which had so intrigued him as a child. It was completely

covered by a banner depicting his own episcopal
coat of arms. School children and whole families
lined the streets. It seemed to be a holiday. All
crowded into the church where Bishop Neumann
spoke to the assembly about the mercies of God,
who had cared for him on his hazardous journeys
and had given him an opportunity to once more
see his family and friends. The formalities having
ended, John Neumann was at last free to go to
see his father.

Refusing to ride, he walked up the well-known
street to the doorway where his father stood.
Clasping his son in his arms the old man in his
excitement lifted him off his feet and carried him
up the steps and into the house.

So great was the crush of family and friends
that his father finally ordered the door closed and
begged his son to dismiss the people by blessing
them from the window through which he used to
give bread.

Each day he was home, the church was packed
at his morning Mass. Great numbers of people
poured into the Neumann home just to speak
to him.

Finally the day to start the return journey to
Philadelphia arrived. Determined not to have
another display, he swore Father Joseph Brunner
to secrecy and requested him to hire a closed
sleigh. Before dawn the next day, he bid good-bye
to his father and sisters.

Rumors had reached him of the farewell
planned, and he was determined to avoid it, even
though he had to disappoint his friends. As the

sleigh reached the mountain ridge, it stopped so he could bid a last farewell to the town he loved so dearly.

Once more he took up the burden of office. All the problems and responsibilities pressed in on him. On his travels homeward he stopped as often as he could to beg for help. Over and over again, to as many as would listen, he told the story of the thousands of immigrants pouring into America and the duty all had to see that these people, poor for the most part, had the consolations of their religion.

"You, who have a church on almost every corner, and can pick and choose your confessors, do not realize what it is to live in such isolation that you may see a priest only every four or five months."

"What can we do to help?" they asked.

"Pray for these missions, send your priests and give alms to help those people in their distress."

So eloquent was he that a number of priests promised to come to America, and he was given substantial sums to help his people.

When he reached Paris he learned that there would be no ship leaving for America until the next month, so he crossed the English Channel, and took a ship from Liverpool. He arrived in New York March 27, 1855.

CHAPTER ELEVEN

CONTEST WITH NATIVISM

BEFORE HE stepped off the ship, Bishop Neumann put on his ring, a sign of his office. Newsboys were hawking their papers on the deck. The headlines were screaming about the Nativist Party.

"America for the Americans," he read as he passed by and wondered ruefully about the ancestors of those who were fomenting trouble.

One of the Redemptorists from New York met him. Under his arm was a newspaper. He took it out to show the bishop the news. "This means trouble," he said.

"These people are worried about their jobs, as the new immigrants pour into the country and are willing to work long hours for less pay," replied the bishop, always trying to see both sides.

"But they are so violent."

"Violence begets violence." A worried frown crossed the bishop's face.

"Counsel your people," he had told his priests before he left for Europe. "Counsel them to be patient and turn the other cheek as Christ taught them. This, too, will pass away."

Although he advocated patience in most cases, he knew that sometimes it was necessary to stand firm against injustice. The mild bishop had stood up for the rights of the church against the trustees of Holy Trinity and had won his case after taking it to the Supreme Court of Pennsylvania. Holy Trinity Church was declared to be the property of the diocese and the judge commanded the trustees to turn over the keys to the building.

When the bishop went to the church, the trustees stood on the steps and refused him entry. He then appealed to the judge who put the men in prison until they complied.

Once again Holy Trinity was opened amidst great rejoicing. Saint Alphonsus Church, which the bishop had hastily erected, thinking the court battle would be long, was almost deserted. The creditors threatened to foreclose.

"Let them foreclose, then you can buy it at a song," advised some people.

"But those creditors, who lent us money in good faith, would lose," he answered. "No, we will find some way to liquidate the debt."

Still influenced by the Nativist movement, the legislature passed the Price Bill which permitted a bishop to hold church property in his name, but forbade it to be left to his successor.

"But, your Lordship, what will happen to church property?" someone asked.

"Until the courts settle this question," replied the bishop, "I will have to bequeath all property to my vicar-general, who in turn will deed it to my successor. It is awkward, but we will survive."

He was more concerned about the clergy who had been infected with the feeling that church property belonged to them personally. Like some other immigrants, a few clerics were opportunists. These men thought they could be laws unto themselves. Bishop Neumann felt keenly that the growth of the church depended on a holy and united clergy.

On October 2, 1855 Bishop Neumann opened the second synod of Philadelphia. It covered every phase of diocesan organization and discipline. In this way he corrected early abuses, such as a case in which the priest's heirs had sold the rectory and made off with the money. In another case, the new pastor found that the dead priest's sister had taken every stick of furniture from the house. From then on, it was understood that anything bought by the parish belonged to the parish.

One of his few joys that year occurred in the spring of 1855. True to his resolve to advise the young women interested in becoming sisters, he met with them one evening. Mary Dorn and Barbara Bell had been living with Mrs. Bachman, a widow, and they had been trying to carry on a community life.

"The Holy Father is greatly interested in you, and would like you to be the first American order of Franciscan sisters. He is a member of the Franciscan order, and you would be closely linked to him."

The smiles on the faces surrounding him told him without words of their happy agreement.

It was decided that the bishop would invite

some Franciscan friars to come to America to help the sisters form their order. The bishop continued his interest in the sisters, even writing their rule by hand. On April 9, 1855 they were invested in the habit of Saint Francis at Saint Peter's Church and a year later took their vows of obedience, chastity and poverty in the bishop's chapel.

Business was just beginning to recover from the depression of 1854-1855. Money was scarce. The summer of 1855 Bishop Neumann called in Father Waldron, who was still struggling to complete the cathedral.

"Father," he said, "we must halt all building."

"But, your Grace, we have no fitting place for you to officiate."

"Saint John's will do very well," replied Bishop Neumann, with an air of finality. "The people are under great financial burdens now. Bread for their children comes first. I will not badger them at this time to give to the cathedral."

Father Waldron left, but talked with his friends about their bad luck in having a bishop not capable of building a cathedral.

The priest was further incensed because at that time the bishop purchased a large plot of land for an orphanage. Father Waldron was not foresighted enough to realize that before the year was out the bishop would be able to sell off some parcels of land and liquidate the debt. Bishop Neumann, however, was not insensitive to the needs for a cathedral. He longed to have a fitting house of God, but he would not go into debt for it. At an annual mass meeting which he inaugurated to further the building of the cathedral he said, "The circumstances of its progressing slowly ought not to discourage anyone, nor should any be tempted to doubt of its ever being finished. Such an assertion would offend Divine Providence. The old saying holds good here. 'What is to last must be built slowly.' Our principal object in moving thus slowly is that the faithful may not be taxed too heavily, since every parish has its own institutions to support."

The May previous to his synod, Bishop Neumann had attended the Eighth Provincial Council in Baltimore. While there, he begged that the bishops petition the pope that his diocese, the largest in the United States, be divided so that it could be better cared for.

"I think," said he, "that the diocese of Philadelphia is too large for any one man to handle well. It should be divided into two dioceses."

"How would you divide it?" asked the Bishop of Pittsburgh.

"I think that Pottsville would make a good center. The bishop could then care for all the souls scattered on the farms and the small towns. So much of my time is wasted on transit from one isolated area to another."

"That would be a poor diocese. Who would want to take that?" asked Archbishop Kenrick doubtfully.

"Oh, I would take the small diocese. I am used to the poor. Then a successor could be appointed to the see of Philadelphia."

The bishops looked at one another in surprise, but they might have known. John Neumann always reserved for himself the most difficult tasks.

Finally, the bishops agreed to Bishop Neumann's idea, and wrote to the pope requesting that the diocese be split.

In Rome the letters of the bishops were weighed carefully. Each of them spoke highly of the bishop's piety and zeal. Archbishop Kenrick, while agreeing to the idea of splitting the diocese, insisted that Bishop Neumann should be retained in Philadelphia.

Bishop O'Connor of Pittsburgh was among the dissenters. Although he considered Bishop Neumann his friend, Bishop O'Connor thought him totally unsuited for the office. The main reasons were that although he was a holy man, he was small in stature and lacking in social grace. So, in a series of letters, he recommended that the bishop be sent to Pottsville. John Neumann, himself, would have been the first to agree with Bishop O'Connor. He had told a friend that "Each day I feel that I am being led to the gallows."

Archbishop Bodini, who was then traveling in the United States as a representative of the pope, made a report on Philadelphia. He said, "The bishop of Philadelphia seems a little inferior for the importance of such a distinguished city, not in learning nor in zeal nor in piety, but because of the littleness of his person and his neglect of the fashions. He is indeed very holy and full of zeal, but more as a missionary than a bishop."

He might have gone to the area administered by Father Kopf in Bellefonte, whose parish covered seven counties. This priest was so poor that he did not own a clerical suit. He wore an old cossack hat and a pair of worn trousers such as a butcher boy would wear. He met the bishop at the train driving a borrowed barouche, a four-wheeled open coach with a box for the driver. It would have been handsome if it were not so ancient that it was about to fall apart. The two horses were so skittish at having to haul such an unaccustomed rig and frightened by the screech of the train that they threatened to bolt.

Bishop Neumann, once settled in the carriage, said, "Father Kopf, my first stop must be Lewistown." There he completely outfitted the priest in a new suit of clothes.

Then they began the hard drive over the Seven Mountains to Bellefonte. The horses were balky. After Confirmation at Bellefonte, they started for Lock Haven, twenty-five miles away. While passing through a covered bridge, a four-horse wagon met them midway. The horses shied and the wagon lurched into the barouche, shattering the shaft. Father Kopf clambered down from his perch on the box and looked at the damage in dismay. The bishop also went to examine the shattered shaft. "I guess there is nothing for it," he said cheerfully, "but you and I will have to play horse."

They tied the horses to the rear of the carriage and pulled it between them. As they neared Lock Haven, Father Kopf, anxious to reach there, increased his pace, but was halted by Bishop

Neumann who said, "If we break down again I won't pull anymore."

Laughing at their plight they came into town, meeting the unbelieving stares of the townsfolk with good humor.

Those who lived in Philadelphia knew nothing about this part of the bishop's life. They only knew that he was away for five to six weeks at a time, and since there was no one else to make decisions, the affairs of the diocese were forced to wait for his return.

Somehow, word was rumored that Bishop Neumann intended to resign. Father Waldron and others who were disgruntled took heart, but the majority of the clergy and laity were uneasy and the poor were distraught. Thus affairs dragged on for two years. Then word came from Rome.

From Bishop Neumann's own reports, and the letters of others, the pope saw that while the diocese had not progressed financially, it had grown spiritually. Instead of transferring Bishop Neumann he assigned him a second or coadjutor bishop to help him run the diocese. The new bishop, Bishop James Wood, was a native Philadelphian, who had been a bank officer in Ohio before becoming a Catholic and a priest.

CHAPTER TWELVE

HELP ARRIVES

BISHOP NEUMANN knew nothing of the rumors of his resignation. All his life he had obeyed rules. There was nothing that would justify him in resigning, so he merely sought a humbler post. He wrote to his friend Father Dichtl: "A new diocese is fraught with certain inconveniences. My long years in the hard service of the church have not only made such misery agreeable but have entirely unfitted me for living as is the vogue in this Babylon of Philadelphia," and he devoutly prayed for a transfer.

The newly appointed bishop, however, had heard the rumors and believed them. He thought that Bishop Neumann would stay only long enough to transfer church property and then would resign, leaving him in full charge. It was under this misapprehension that he accepted the post.

Bowing, as always, to the will of authority, Bishop Neumann was delighted that he would have help in his work. He had not the slightest idea what was in the mind of his new coadjutor.

The first word of his assistant's upcoming

consecration came from a secular newspaper and he wrote to Archbishop Kenrick for confirmation. Along with the rector of the seminary and two other priests he journeyed to Cincinnati for Bishop Wood's consecration. He met his new coadjutor for the first time in April, 1857.

To welcome the new bishop, a committee was formed to make sure that everything possible was done to honor him. What he refused for himself, Bishop Neumann was always eager to provide for others.

"My dear bishop," said Bishop Neumann as they sat in his office on the day they returned home, "you can't imagine how delighted I am to have you with me."

"I hope I can be of service," murmured the new bishop.

"Certainly, certainly," replied Bishop Neumann with enthusiasm. "How would you like to care for the financial end of our affairs?"

Bishop Wood's face lit up. "It would please me greatly to put the affairs of the diocese in order."

"No more than it would please me," replied Bishop Neumann with a faint smile.

With good will, Bishop Wood worked to put the finances on a firm business basis. He did so well that during the crisis of 1857 the church did not suffer and those who regularly invested their savings in church societies never lost a cent. The tall handsome new bishop found the administration of most of the affairs in the city greatly to his liking.

In his turn, however, he found Father Waldron

using every means to force him to complete the cathedral. At last he said, "Since you are so unhappy with my decisions, I suggest you apply for a transfer to another diocese." Bishop Neumann had not dealt so harshly with the troublemaker.

Unhappy about the continued presence of the bishop, the newly appointed coadjutor wrote letters to his friends complaining about his superior. In a letter to the archbishop of Cincinnati, he wrote, "Bishop Neumann is out of town and leaves me to fight the financial battles singlehanded; which is perhaps as well, for he has such little skill in these matters, that if he did essay a blow, it would be full as likely to knock me down as anyone else."

Bishop Wood seemed to forget the years in which his superior had handled the affairs for all the diocese and yet kept it afloat.

In 1857, to Bishop Neumann's great delight, his nephew John Berger arrived in Philadelphia from Prachatitz. He met him at the train and immediately took him to his home on Logan Square. Another member of his family would devote his life to the cause so dear to his heart, the poor in America.

"Now tell me, how were the family when you left? Your grandfather is well? Your mother and aunts?"

He treasured all accounts of the family. "It seems like ten years instead of two since I have seen them. You know, I will never see them again in this life," he said.

Young John Berger intended to become a parish priest, so his uncle sent him to the seminary at Latrobe for some preparatory training. That summer he took his nephew on his parish visitation to introduce him to missionary life.

One incident especially remained in the young man's mind. The priest met them at the train and went in search of a carriage. The only conveyance he could muster was a manure cart. Over the back he placed a plank. The bishop and young John sat on the plank with their legs dangling almost to the ground and their bags beside them. On the way to their destination rain began to fall. They were soaked and the steaming manure added to their discomfort. The bishop turned to his nephew and said, "John, did you ever see a bishop in such an entourage?"

Huddled against the rain, the young man observed, "Bishops in America are not like bishops in Europe."

Having visited the coal mines and seen the unrest, the bishop was disturbed at the threat posed by the new secret society, the Molly Maguires. He preached against them, and his people listened for a while. It was not until after his death that the Molly Maguires caused so much death and destruction.

His desire for good education led Bishop Neumann to invite a number of religious communities into the diocese. In 1855, the Jesuits opened a college. Villanova College was strengthened by his support, and the Christian brothers conducted a school for boys.

The order of nuns who came to the diocese included the Good Shepherd sisters, the Sisters of Notre Dame de Namur, Holy Cross, Immaculate Heart of Mary, and Saint Joseph. To each he offered his spiritual help, urging them to call on him with any problem. Through some technicality, his own sister and the Sisters of Saint Charles never came from Bohemia.

The Sisters of Saint Joseph staffed a hospital, taught school and established their motherhouse in Chestnut Hill, a suburb of Philadelphia. Bishop Neumann was a frequent visitor, giving advice to the young nuns. He gave to the sisters the chalice which had been presented to him when he visited the seminary in Prague in 1855. On the cup and base were woven a handsome floral design. On the base, the inscription told that it had been wrought almost two hundred years previously for a Father Peter Kearney, a professor at the University of Prague.

With a wry smile, he said to Mother Saint John, when he presented the chalice, "See, Mother, Bohemia had a college when America was still a wilderness." It could be that he had heard insinuations that Bohemians were less cultured than native Americans.

When Father Waldron left the diocese, Bishop Wood took over the building of the cathedral. By 1858 the facade was up. On September 13, 1859, the keystone was set and the cross placed in position atop the dome. With great ceremony, Bishop Wood blessed the cathedral, and Bishop Neumann presided. There was still much to be done to the interior before it could be brought to completion.

The bishop, however, had a treasure that he was saving for display in the cathedral. It was a three-foot-tall crucifix of solid ivory which had been given to him a few years previously. It had been carved by an untutored monk in Genoa. One day in a vision the monk saw our Lord hanging from the cross, and was filled with the desire to reproduce the vision. In the storeroom of the monastery was a piece of ivory, three feet long, fourteen inches thick and weighing about 125 pounds. The monk received permission to use it, and for four years labored to recreate his vision. The result was claimed to be a masterpiece. In 1843 an American consul bought it from the monastery. It was brought to the United States and given to Bishop Neumann, who kept it in trust for his people of Philadelphia. Unfortunately this crucifix was stolen from the cathedral some time after Bishop Neumann's death.

Realizing that the glory of the church rested on its leaders, the bishop spent much time and thought in promoting a strong and holy priesthood. He established a junior seminary and was most generous about giving retreats for priests.

Bishop Timon in Buffalo invited him to give a retreat in his diocese. The first evening of the retreat one of the priests came to him and in halting English told him that he and several other German priests were not fluent enough in English to follow his sermons.

"That is easily remedied," replied Bishop

Neumann, "I will give you the exercises in German an hour later." Thus he preached six times each day during the ten-day retreat.

"Come to see me any time. My door is always open," he said over and over again to his priests. No priest had to make an appointment for an interview.

One day his nephew John came to see him. "And how are you today, my boy?" he asked.

"Fine, now, Uncle, since I have come to a decision. I am to follow in your footsteps and become a Redemptorist."

Delighted, Bishop Neumann clasped the young man on the shoulder. "Just don't follow too far and become a bishop. I could not wish that for you."

Happy at the arrangement for the division of labor, Bishop Neumann continued in ignorance of his coadjutor's disappointment.

Finally, word reached him of the misapprehension under which Bishop Wood had accepted the post.

Making a special appointment to speak in private he said, "I am distressed that you were under the wrong impression in coming to Philadelphia."

Embarrassed, Bishop Wood did not know how to reply. "You well know I would be happy to turn over to you this diocese, but the pope has given me no choice. There is no valid reason I can offer for resigning. At the upcoming Provincial Council I will once again petition for a division of the diocese but in the meantime, I am afraid you will have to put up with me." Not to upset his coadjutor further, he rose and walked from the room.

At the next Provincial Council, Bishop Neumann asked again that the diocese be split, and he be given the less important one. More bishops, having heard that Bishop Neumann had many critics in Philadelphia, were willing to petition the pope to accept his suggestion. Once again, nothing came of it. Word came that the decision would be deferred until the next Baltimore Council.

Even though he was aware that his coadjutor was antagonistic to him, Bishop Neumann went about his business as though nothing were amiss. He continued his parish visitations of the outlying districts, leaving the city and its problems to Bishop Wood. The sisters, especially those recently established in the diocese, received his loving care.

While visiting one convent, the mother told him of their financial plight. They did not have any money in the house. "I regret that I have no money to finance you on a regular basis," he said, "but," and he thrust his hand into a pocket, "here are some Yankee medals which may help," and he dropped some gold coins into the mother's hand.

He was delighted to be able to write his father that "Last summer, twenty churches were built and paid for out of collections. Six are for Germans." Progress was being made.

CHAPTER THIRTEEN

BELOVED OF GOD

NOW THAT all the work did not fall on his shoulders the bishop found an extra hour or two to spend at Saint Peter's with his fellow Redemptorists. A priest recently arrived from Europe walked into the recreation room one day and saw a knot of priests surrounding a small man in a shabby suit. "Is this what they do in America? Allow strangers into their cloister? How odd!" he thought.

At that moment someone called him over and said, "Your Lordship, may I present our newest addition from Germany?" So this was the famous Bishop Neumann. He certainly did not look the part.

One day, while drying dishes in the kitchen at Saint Peter's, he asked the lay brother whether he preferred a sudden or a lingering death. The lay brother thought that a lingering illness might help him prepare better for his last end.

"You may be right, brother, but I think," said Bishop Neumann, "a Christian, and still more a religious, should always be prepared for a good death, and in that case a sudden one is not with-

137

out its advantages. It spares us, as well as our attendants, many a temptation to impatience; besides, the devil has not so much time to trouble us. In either case, however, the death that God sends is the best for us."

One wonders if he had a premonition of his own end.

The Christmas season of 1859-1860 was as busy as usual. Christmas day, Bishop Wood presided in the new cathedral, while Bishop Neumann presided at Saint John's Church, where he preached. He had spent long hours in the confessional on Christmas Eve.

On January 4th, he wrote a friend, "I am not feeling well these days." That was a most unusual admission for him to make.

At lunch with Bishop Wood at Logan Square on January 5th, he enlivened the conversation by repeating an anecdote from his early days. "As I was about to leave Prachatitz," he related, "an old man came to me and pressed two gold coins into my hand. 'John,' he said, 'as soon as you get aboard the ship, slip these coins into the captain's hand and say to him, "Now Captain, always steer your ship close to the land." When he does that, if the ship is wrecked, you can save yourself by swimming to shore.'"

Relaxed, they left the table. Shortly thereafter, Father Urban, long a friend of his, called on the bishop, who seemed scarcely to recognize him. Noting that his eyes looked glassy, the priest inquired for his health.

"I feel as I never felt before. It is a strange

feeling," he answered. "But the air will do me good. I must go on several errands." Although uneasy, Father Urban left, and the bishop prepared to go out. The day was cold, there was a penetrating wind, and the streets were covered with ice and snow. First he walked to the parcels office to inquire about a chalice that he had consecrated and sent to Father Kopf, but which had never arrived. Then he went to see his lawyer about some papers. Returning, he crossed Vine near Thirteenth Street. Someone noted that his step was uncertain. Reaching the foot path, he collapsed. Two men rushed up and carried him into the parlor of a Mr. Quein, and there he died, as he had often slept, on the floor. Word spread through the diocese, and the bishop's death was announced at all Masses the next day, the feast of the Epiphany.

The following Sunday, his former vicar-general and faithful friend Father Sourin preached about the virtues of the bishop. He said, "It is now eight years since the bishop came among us. From the first day to the moment of his death, the period has been one of labor and suffering. He knew very well, my dear brethern, that in this city there were many who wished, as an occupant for the episcopate of this diocese, a man more according to the judgment and tastes of the world. . . . There was not in these United States a priest or a bishop superior in zeal for souls."

Those who did not venerate him in life gave him all the honors they could at death. The humble little man had a funeral such as never had been seen in the city. Archbishop Kenrick, his ardent supporter, preached at the funeral Mass.

It is customary for a bishop to be buried in his cathedral, but the provincial of the Redemptorists petitioned that Bishop Neumann be buried at Saint Peter's Church. Archbishop Kenrick agreed, saying, "I will gladly consent to Bishop Neumann's finding after death a restingplace where he sought it in life but could not find it."

Six days after his death, services were held in Saint Peter's Church. The appearance of the bishop had not changed. His body was as flexible in death as it had been in life.

His city of Prachatitz decided to hold solemn services for its distinguished son. In the cemetery, on the lot belonging to the Neumann family, the city erected a metal statue of the Blessed Virgin under the title of The Immaculate Conception. On the base, after noting his birth and death, the inscription read, "This Monument was Erected by his Faithful Friends."

And the bishop did have faithful friends who came time and again to visit his grave. Gradually word came of miraculous cures of the body. No one could count the cures of the spirit.

While still alive, several instances of prophecy had been attributed to him. He had said to his nephew, "My father is now eighty. I will not live to be fifty." He was not yet forty-nine when he died. There is another account of a widow who took her two-year-old son to see the bishop. "He suffers agonizing pain with dropsy of the head," she told him. "They tell me he must die soon." Laying his hand on the child's head, the kind bishop said, "This child will not die. He will grow into manhood and be your consolation and your joy." And so it turned out.

On the thirtieth day after the bishop's death, the vault was opened and the coffin raised. The body was found perfectly incorrupt. Ten months later, the process was repeated. This time decomposition had set in.

Devotion to the cause of Bishop Neumann grew. Cures, large and small were effected. In order for them to be declared miraculous, the church subjects them to the most careful scrutiny.

In 1886, Archbishop Ryan of Philadelphia began an investigation of his predecessor's virtues. After eleven years' study by local clergy, the case was sent to Rome. Thirty years later, in 1921, after examination of his writing and interviews of those who had known him, Pope Benedict XV solemnly declared that John Neumann was an example of outstanding virtue and therefore should be venerated.

The first step had been taken towards canonization. Cures followed. Eva Benassi, an Italian girl, was cured of peritonitis after praying to him. This event happened only two years after he was declared venerable, the first step towards canonization. Another case was of a Villanova boy, J. Kent Lenahan, who had been crushed in an automobile accident, and was considered beyond hope. A piece of the bishop's cassock was applied to him. He miraculously recovered.

In 1930, the Neumann League of Prayer was established in Philadelphia, and the devotion quickly spread to other parts of the nation. This was succeeded in 1958 by the Venerable Neumann Guild, whose main purpose was to pray for God's manifestation, through miracles performed, that the bishop is a saint, this being the criteria by which the church can be sure that a person has found special favor in the sight of God.

Cardinal, then Archbishop, Krol was appointed to the see of Philadelphia on the 150th anniversary of John Neumann's birth. Impressed by the holiness of his predecessor's life, he has worked for the acknowledgment of his sainthood.

Because of the incontrovertible evidence of the cures of Eva Benassi and J. Kent Lenahan, the Sacred Congregation for the Cause of Saints declared the miracles valid. In 1963, Pope John XXIII declared the bishop Blessed and he was formally beatified by Pope Paul VI on October 13, 1963.

The next step in the long process of canonization was the examination of another miracle that could without doubt be attributed to the bishop. The authorities examined the case of a New Jersey boy. Michael Flannigan, when nine years old, developed bone cancer as the result of a fall. He was subjected to all the modern treatment—drugs, radiation, operations; none was effective. His parents then took the boy to the shrine of Bishop Neumann in Saint Peter's Church. Prayers were offered, and a relic was applied to the cancer. The symptoms completely disappeared. The Congregation for the Causes of the Saints declared that there was no natural medical or scientific explanation. This decision has caused Pope Paul VI to declare that Bishop John Neumann is a saint.

Thus, to the satisfaction of all, it can readily be seen that the prayer offered to God by John Neumann at his first Mass, "Dearest God, Give me Holiness" has been heard and answered.

BIBLIOGRAPHY

Berger, Rev. John A., C.SS.R. *Life of Right Reverend John N. Neumann, D.D. of the Congregation of the Most Holy Redeemer. Fourth Bishop of Philadelphia.* Translated from the German by Rev. Eugene Grimm, C.SS.R. 2nd ed. New York, Benziger, 1884. 475 p. port.

Curley, Rev. Michael J., C.SS.R. *Venerable John Neumann, C.SS.R., Fourth Bishop of Philadelphia.* Philadelphia, Bishop Neumann Center, 1952. XV, 547 p. port. illus.

Finnegan, Charles V., O.F.M. *Priest's Manual for the Forty Hours Devotion.* Paterson, N.J. St. Anthony Guild Press, c.1958. XL, 92 p.

Frean, Rev. W., C.SS.R. *Blessed John Neumann; the Helper of the Afflicted.* Ballarat, Australia, Majellan Press, c.1963. XL, 288 p. port.

Kirlin, Joseph. *Catholicity in Philadelphia.* Philadelphia, John Joseph McVey, 1909. XV, 546 p. ports.

GENERAL WORKS

Album of American History. N.Y. Scribner, 1969. 6 Vol. illus. V.2 1783-1853.

American Heritage Pictorial Atlas of U.S. History. New York, American Heritage Publishing Company, c.1966. 424 p. illus.

Makers of America. Chicago, Encylopaedia Britannica Educational Corporation, 1971. Vol. 2 Builders of a New Nation, 1801-1848.

PERIODICALS

American Catholic Historical Society. Records 37:
100-3; 41:1-26; 162-192; 263ff; 42:285-292
American Catholic History Researches. 26:289; 28:
211, 313; 341-4; 29:41
National Geographic. 31:163-187

NEWSPAPERS

Catholic Standard and Times. 12-25-75:17:3ff; 2-10-
76:25; 3-18-76:19

FURTHER READING

Adams, James Truslow. *Album of American History.*
New York, Scribner, c.1969. volume 2 1783-1853.

Boorstin, Daniel J. *Landmark History of the American People from Plymouth to Appomattox.* New
York, Random, c.1968. 185 p. illus.

Carmer, Carl, ed. *Cavalcade of America.* New York,
Crown, c.1956. 382 p. illus.

Connelly, James F. Ed. *The History of the Archdiocese of Philadelphia.* Philadelphia Archdiocese,
c.1976. p. ports. illus.

Eiseman, Alberta. *From Many Lands.* New York,
Atheneum, 1970. 216 p. illus.

Hoff, Rhoda. *America,* New York, Walck, 1962. 167
p. illus.

Lewis, Arthur H. *Lament of the Molly Maguires.*
New York, Harcourt, 1964. 308 p.

Meadowcroft, Enid La Monte. *Land of the Free.*
New York, Crowell, c.1961. 151 p. illus.

Morris, Richard B. *Voice from America's Past.* New
York, Dutton, c.1963. volume 2 *Backwoods Democrary to World Power.*

Ogg, Frederic Austin. *Pageant of America.* New
Haven, Yale University Press, 1927. volume 8
Builders of the Republic.